T0147610

THE PAGANS ARE REVOLTING

s. d. lake

iUniverse, Inc.
New York Bloomington

The Pagans Are Revolting

iUniverse books may be ordered through booksellers or by contacting:

iUniverse
1663 Liberty Drive
Bloomington, IN 47403
www.iuniverse.com
1-800-Authors (1-800-288-4677)

ISBN: 978-1-4502-4389-6 (sc)
ISBN: 978-1-4502-4391-9 (dj)
ISBN: 978-1-4502-4390-2 (ebook)

Printed in the United States of America

iUniverse rev. date: 08/04/2010

To my wife Paulette without whom this endeavor would have never come to completion.

All honor and glory be to the God and Father of our Lord Jesus Christ.

Contents

SECTION III

Preface

In some segments of society within the United States of America at this present time (early in 2010), there is a concerted effort to fundamentally change the foundations of this society to mimic European socialism. In order for this effort to succeed, two things must change: (1) Christianity and Jesus Christ must be demonized and discredited as hate mongers, and (2) any reference to God and the faith of the founding fathers of the Constitution of the United States must be rewritten or minimized as to having influenced the writing of the Constitution. This strategy has been in play now for over seventy-five years, stretching back to the 1930s. It has been bearing fruit since the 1960s, and the final onslaught is only now beginning to materialize within the court systems and educational systems of the United States.

The United States House of Representatives has been sufficiently corrupted, along with the Senate, to give voice to many anti-Christian policies and to restrain any "religious" influences within the society in regard to laws governing the behavior of its citizens. This is to the demise of much of the upcoming generation, who now believe that values and morals are relative to the individual and any given situation.

In these writings, it is my hope to bring a bright light to bear on some of the antecedents of this polluted culture that some elitist socialist thinkers have forced upon U.S. citizens against their will. Many of these elite socialist thinkers have slithered their way into positions of power in order to reinvent the United States to fit their idealistic notions of a social harmony where all personal behavior and attitudes are on equal footing in the arena of moral correctness and personal choice apart from any Christian foundational influence yet embracing a pagan ideology of an acceptance of animalistic evolutionary behaviors.

It is not too late to put things right, but the time is *now* and the method is the ballot box. Good people need to get their thinking straight about what they stand for in the area of healthy behavior and proper respect for themselves. They also need to consider what is being implanted in the next generation so that our children may grow up in a country that is indeed a light to the rest of the world in regard to real freedom and the pursuit of real happiness and not as some decadent counterfeit that is based in debauchery and no self-restraint from momentary excitement masquerading as real contentment and fulfillment. Chaos is not freedom at all; it just leads to long-term destruction.

It is my intent to awaken a sense of urgency and encourage people to take a stand *right now* to rid America of this creeping cancer before it becomes terminal to our children and grandchildren.

Sincerely,
S.D. Lake

Section I

"Citizens, by birth or choice, of a common country, that country has a right to concentrate your affections. The name of American, which belongs to you in your national capacity, must always exalt the just pride of patriotism more than any appellation derived from local discriminations. With slight shades of difference, you have the same religion, manners, habits, and political principles. You have in a common cause fought and triumphed together; the independence and liberty you possess are the work of joint counsels, and joint efforts of common dangers, sufferings, and successes"

(Washington, 1796)

Chapter 1

The Pagans Are Revolting: United States Overrun from Within

Who?

The pagans, that's who! What is a pagan, you might ask, and why do I think they are revolting? Well, in a way, I guess the term *pagan* could be subjective, or as some say, "in the eye of the beholder," much like what constitutes "art." The dictionary describes a *pagan* as someone who does not believe in a Supreme Being or God, specifically the God of the Judeo-Christian tradition on which Western culture—until lately—was and in some instances still is based with its code of law and morality. Therein lies considerable friction with certain individuals who do not want any restraints on personal behavior or choices regarding how people choose to live their lives. They live by the old "it ain't nobody's business but my own" mantra.

So why are pagans revolting? Why do they arouse feelings of disgust and repulsion? The way the filth of their unrestrained lifestyle demands flies in the face of good law and decent morals is revolting, not to mention the destruction of a healthy society because of the pagan belief system's self-centeredness and its lack of any concept of duty to the whole of society.

A slow seeping of sewage is now a flood

Much like the slow seeping of diseased matter into a lake of drinking water will eventually pollute the whole body of life-giving substance, so has the perversion of our educational system destroyed the moral roots of America and the ideology it was founded on. This is no accident; it was and still is the goal of the secular humanistic movement in American society. The saying "bring back the lions" is not meant as a joke; secular humanists, in collaboration with pagan philosophy, truly want to kill off all references to Christianity within American culture. And just like the Nazi political party in Germany destroyed Germany by using its own constitution against it, so too are the pagans and secularist also destroying America.

Under the myth of freedom from religion, they are turning the freedom that our Judeo-Christian Constitution represents against itself in a perversion of turning freedom *of* religion into freedom *from* religion. They truly are revolting, and they are stealing the next generation of Americans right out from under Christian believers in American. They are corrupting the Christian children against their parents in state and private universities and colleges; professors of death (the pseudo Gestapo) are running our educational systems at this point, and their teachings have seeped into every vestige of decency in American society. Just look at the news of the day on any given day.

What constitutes a religion?

According to the *Encarta World English Dictionary*, religion is defined as follows:

re-li-gion [ri lijjsn] (plural re-li-gions) n

1. beliefs and worship: people's beliefs and opinions concerning the existence, nature, and worship of a deity or deities, and divine involvement in the universe and human life.
2. system: an institutionalized or personal system of beliefs and practices relating to the divine.
3. personal beliefs or values: a set of strongly-held beliefs, values, and attitudes that somebody lives by.

4. obsession: an object, practice, cause, or activity that somebody is completely devoted to or obsessed by.
5. The danger is that you start to make fitness a religion.
6. Christianity monk's or nun's life: life as a monk or a nun, especially in the Roman Catholic Church.

As you can see from the second and third definitions, secularism and naturalism as well as atheism have indeed become religious ways of thinking. It has become fashionable to be anti anything that supports Judeo-Christian values. You may ask what the Jews have to do with anything in regard to this present age of paganism. Well, you know Judaism has been an established religion for numerous centuries and can stand alone without Christianity. Christianity, on the other hand, cannot stand without Judaism and the foundational beliefs about God and His Son, which the Christian doctrine of redemption are founded on, as well as the moral absolutes that much of American law and established societal norms are also founded on. Pagans want to rewrite the laws and moral codes that govern society so they suit self-absorbed, self-indulgent lifestyles that will only lead to a society that offers no boundaries to guide its citizens to healthy and righteous lives.

The whole argument is over who will set a standard to guide lawmaking or moral codes. Will the standard be set by non-Christian people who make up their own moral codes based on personal preferences? Or will it be set by Christian individuals, who base their codes on established codes of conduct for society, which in turn are based on a moral code of freedom within boundaries that protect individuals from one another and help society move forward in its pursuit of better lives for all its citizens? Some people think that no restraints on behavior are a good thing for individuals; they want to live like dogs, with the same moral code as animals. After all, secular humanists and pagans keep pushing the belief that humans are nothing more than unique animals on this globe we call Earth. They would have us believe that we are nothing special and certainly not made in the image of any Creator.

In your face

Recently, the national headlines in the media revealed the fact that young adults in a high school in New Jersey were sending naked pictures of themselves to their friends via their cell phones. It seems this is a common practice these days. When a local district attorney (DA) threatened these individuals with child pornography laws for their behavior, the American Civil Liberties Union (ACLU—should read the American Communist Lawyers Union) filed suit against the DA, saying those laws didn't apply to young people under the age of eighteen and could not be used to prosecute them. That's interesting. Eleven- and twelve-year-olds are having sexual intercourse in school classrooms while their friends stand watch in the hallways, but that isn't actually against the law either as long as both parties are willingly consenting, are no more than four years apart in age, and are both under eighteen.

On April 1, 2009, in my local paper—*Pocono Record*, Stroudsburg, Pennsylvania (Pocono Record, 2009)—there was an article about an investigation into allegations made by young girls on the elementary school bus that eleven-year-old boys were "pulling down their pants and exposing themselves to the ten-year-old girls and threatening to take them home and 'hump' them." They also claimed that the boys also used other foul language and sexually explicit suggestions. These are the children in public school!

The Children & Youth Services (CYS) should be investigating these families and finding out what these children are being exposed to in their homes. But of course these children cannot be taught any moral values in the school system because these so-called "values" are a subjective assumption and as such are presumed to be religious in nature.

This nonsense has been going on since the 1960s (that cohort group from the new enlightened secular theologians) with secular humanists. The ethics are subjective group (no moral absolutes) have been running the school system, so it is no wonder the mess Wall Street and the banking industry find themselves in; it is not surprising with these kind of moral leaders running the show. It truly is an anything-goes society we have going here in America, and if you stand up for Christian values, you are called a narrow-minded, intolerant individual.

The school systems in many parts of our country are turning our children and grandchildren into nothing but little dogs. I guess they truly do need to hand out condoms to students; I mean, you can't actually have them fixed—yet. All this sludge is on a slippery slope alright.

It can be understood why pagans are trying to get rid of parental consent for underage abortions; they want school guidance counselors to be able to drive students down to a clinic between their classes at school when the condoms don't get the job done. It is in the agenda that birth control pills be distributed as part of the health and hygiene classes in fourth grade. Don't laugh. Parents will go along with it as long as it is paid for by the states, and if anyone complains, they will be ridiculed as promoting unwanted juvenile pregnancy. The abortion industry (Planned Parenthood) won't like it much either; passing out birth control will cut into the profits of the abortion industry—those who see abortion as a viable option for world population control.

You know, I have been rethinking my stand on the abortion issue lately and have come to the conclusion that if an aborted child goes immediately into heaven as Christians believe, then let the pagans abort their offspring. They won't be able to raise another generation of godless children. In the Old Testament of Christian scripture it simply says not to throw your "children" into the fire like the pagans do. It doesn't say to get the pagans to stop throwing their children into the fires (Deuteronomy 18:10, NKJV).

The Constitution was written for moral people, and it is woefully inadequate to protect people from those who have no morals, those who have corrupted the rule of law, and those who want a society predicated on greed, genitals, and self-indulgence. When anything is conceptualized as religious simply because it sets a standard for human behavior and when all religious views should supposedly be kept separate from government, then what is left on which to base a judgment for societal rules? Absolutely nothing but humanistic jargon and naturalistic urges.

Now it is a popular notion and it has been heard that pedophiles are now saying they shouldn't be punished for their behavior because they are "born" that way—born with a tendency toward preadolescent children for personal sexual gratification. And if it is a consenting situation, they ask why there is punishment for such behavior. After all, the age of consent is just an arbitrary number based on religious beliefs, just like marriage is based on religious beliefs. They ask, why can't a man—or a woman for that matter—have more than one so-called legal mate or partner? Or once individuals reach puberty, why is age an issue?

Why are Christian children such easy prey for secular humanists?

So many people have such good intentions while raising their children in a proper way. They want their kids to be good citizens in a society that strives to have all its citizens living free from oppression and unjust laws. They send them to schools that are not "secular" in nature, and they teach them that there are rights and wrongs when it comes to behavior. They teach them that they shouldn't just live for themselves and that other people matter too. They tell their kids there are things like honesty, character, integrity, and fidelity and that these things have in themselves their own reward when practiced diligently with no compromise.

They also give their Christian training in a Christian worldview—a view that there is a God, that He is the Creator of everything, that we humans were separated from Him long ago because of sin, and that we now need someone to pay the price for our lawlessness—the penalty for which being death—so that we don't have to die ourselves and be forever separated from Him in His realm. In order to do this, we have to accept the death of His Son as our own payment for our disobedience, and in that way our debt is paid and we are once again restored to His favor and blessings. This is the story of the Gospel, and the Christian writings and scripture go straight to the point of the issue.

There is more than enough evidence that points to the truth of what the Christian worldview proclaims. It is recorded throughout history, and the proof is in the pudding, so to speak, from those who have lived it and experienced the presence of God the Father of the Lord Jesus Christ in their lives when they yielded their self-centered desires and self-gratifying spirit over to His direction and presence and lived according to His concepts and precepts. In other words, do the right thing simply because it is the right thing to do and you will automatically reap a reward and ignite the power to pull the blessings of God into your life.

For young people to understand this is not hard when they are raised in a truly Christian family atmosphere; it is not a surprise for them to hear this proclaimed. One needs to be careful of what other "truths" children are told. There are some Christian groups that teach some things that don't have any bearing on the Good News in general but have a bearing on the credibility of the Christian worldview in general. It is like you get a bunch of information from a source and much of it sounds reasonable, yet it is epistemological in nature and the general understanding is that it makes good sense. However, in with this logical hypothesis of the subject, there is some information that will be shown later to be absolutely false as originally presented. Upon further review, it is found that the reality of the subject matter shows what was once believed cannot possibly be the way it was presented, yet some individuals believe that if we were to change our understanding of this particular subject matter, it would somehow cast doubt on the truth of the rest of the material that was presented along with it. I would say that this is not always the case.

For example, there was a time when the whole worldview was that the earth was the center of the universe and that all other objects in the universe revolved around the earth—the sun, moon, planets, and stars. Of course, at the time people said that was what God's Word in Christian scriptures stated. Not so. The misinterpretations of the scriptures led to many false beliefs. The truth—that the earth revolves around the sun—didn't make the scriptures inaccurate; it simply showed that the translators made some errors in their thinking while trying to translate original scriptures into the English language. It is not an unusual occurrence when dealing with ancient languages. When evidence shows something is not lining up, one simply needs to update the translations into a more accurate form than they were originally understood to mean.

God's Word is true. There are no fairy tales here, or legends or wives tales, just *facts* centered in reality. The realities of this physical world do not contradict the description of how and when the universe was created in the first book of the Christian scriptures. It is an old universe and an old earth, and the Word says just that. If we continue to teach our children erroneous facts based on bad translations, they will be "low-hanging fruit" for the pagans—very easy to pick off the tree of family beliefs and values. To believe the earth is very old and ancient is *not* the same as having a belief in Darwin's evolution theory. The earth and universe can be very old, and this belief does not compromise the reality of the one true God of the Christian faith—the God and Father of the Lord and Savior Jesus Christ. Those that posit that the contrary is true, that it *does* compromise the Christian faith, are extremely ignorant and dogmatic to the destruction of the truth of the Christian worldview. Go to www.reason.org to establish some realistic attitudes regarding the ancient text.

God's Word lines up with His world!

Now you know why convicted felons are not allowed to vote

If convicted felons could vote, they would vote other like-minded individuals into public office—others with little regard for the rule of law as the foundation for a just and honest society. Then they would be able to make unjust laws that could/would take advantage of the other citizens within the society. They would be able to discard opposing opinions and suggestions that are based on duty and honor as to how the society should be run.

This is pretty much what is going on today with a large group of pagan individuals voting for and electing people of like-mindedness to overturn the foundations of the American society, which were decidedly based on Christian values. I understand that there have always been the few throughout history who made it into areas of public trust and have gone on to show themselves to not be worthy of that trust. Today, people proclaim to be pagans, and they appeal to others who want no moral restraints on their lives, businesses, or personal relationships.

It was recently in the news that a women wanted to "legally" marry a porpoise because she had fallen in love with it. Others want to marry many different people at the same time. Still others want to have the right to have sex with anything that breathes, without being judged by others regarding their moral standing within society. The issue is not about marriage. Don't kid yourself. They don't want to be like those who enter into a legal, religiously inspired marriage. They just want to be able to say marriage doesn't mean anything. After all, everybody is married to something or somebody.

So as pagans begin to take over the public arena with their ideology, before you know it they are making educational rules, determining what you can and cannot say about morality in a society, and determining what you can and cannot say about the behavior of others in society.

However, many people feel there is a standard we should all live by, and that standard has some basis in a Christian moral worldview, with an attitude about limits and parameters set with wisdom and forethought. Pagans, on the other hand, want to make up laws and acceptable behavior limits as they go along because there is always some new experience on the horizon that they might want to try. If you don't agree with their humanistic views, they deem what you say as "hate speech."

There recently was a fellow who died after he allowed his horse—that's right, his *horse*—to have anal sex with him. Believe it or not, his friends felt so very sorry that he'd had a bad experience after having this relationship with his "best friend" (he died from internal complications) that they made a movie showing his behavior in a favorable light. Bestiality is making a comeback in society after it was strictly on the taboo list for many societies for many centuries. Now it is fashionable to do things that are "taboo" or to live a "nontraditional" lifestyle—or, in other words, a "perverted" lifestyle. A lifestyle that is set against all the centuries of wisdom that have brought Western culture into its most productive and healthiest era in recorded human history. Now if that only applies to the "Christian" industrial countries of the world, then look at the political systems of the third world countries to see where the problems lie.

In third world countries, there is no rule of a just law system; political systems are corrupt. America is becoming corrupt in its thinking at the highest levels of public service and political office. Leaders, those with political and organizational power, no longer take their vows of office or company directives seriously. They think the ends justify the means, and their end goal has been perverted through the perversion of the educational system that has brought them to where they are today; few remain who have been educated in a correct Christian theological manner regarding ethics and morals. These leaders are pagans and secular humanists for the most part, and they are turning our society into a pagan society, not a secular society but a pagan society. The dogs are loose, and the dog catchers have all been fired because they thought wild dogs should be controlled. My heart goes out to the upcoming generations. They won't even know what they have lost because they will have never seen the goodness of a moral society. They will probably be too busy going to state-sponsored orgies and drug parties cosponsored by the leading soft drink manufacture of the era. After all, everything you see in the advertising venue these days has a sexual innuendo or some reference to bodily functions that is considered witty and cute.

This brings me back to why it is so important that Christian children are not raised in some make-believe concept of the realities of this physical existence. As the pagans will most probably abort most of their children, it will become more and more imperative that they steal the Christian children and shape them into the citizens they want to make the rules of law. Christian children need to know that their faith is not based on some nice fairy tale of make-believe; they need to know that the creation of the universe, the development of the earth, the creation of all life, and specifically the creation of the human race are clearly explained in the book of Genesis, chapters 1–2 and many other areas of the Judeo-Christian scriptures.

The observable scientific explanation of the creation lines up perfectly with the sequence of events described in the Bible. Make no mistake about it, if Christian children are continually told mythical style like biblical children's stories that are just shadows of the truth, their faith will begin to seem like a fairy tale in itself, the Gospel Story will seem just like it is indeed only a story. Then the pagans will turn them into secular humanists, which will create deadly consequences for them and the future of the American society.

> *Only the Judeo-Christian tradition contains worship of an infinite personal being.*
>
> —Francis Schaeffer

Chapter 2

Stinkin' Thinkin': A Learned Deception of Erroneous Beliefs

A letter to the Colossians

> *See to it that no one carries you off as spoil or makes you yourselves captive by his so-called philosophy and intellectualism and vain deceit (idle fancies and plain nonsense), following human tradition (men's ideas of the material rather than the spiritual world), just crude notions following the rudimentary and elemental teachings of the universe and disregarding [the teachings of] Christ (the Messiah). (Col. 2:8 AMP)*
>
> Are *you* a believer in the reality of Christ?

Filed in the darkness of the last row

What is in a thought? That kind of sounds as if there is an ingredient list for our mental processes, as if thoughts are made up of substances, such as wood, iron, steel, plastic, Styrofoam, or the like. What is the reality of the process? Are our thoughts generated by chemical reactions, our cerebral activity? Or are those chemical reactions generated by our thoughts? What makes a person think? Is it the outside stimulus triggering our physical senses that makes us act and react in very specific ways? If stimulus is received in a very subjective way, then how we perceive the stimulus (i.e., think about what we see and feel) will determine our reaction to that stimulus.

So what do we as individuals base our assumptions or guiding principles and beliefs on?

The human mind is a field of dreams or nightmares. It depends on what is planted; it is the seed that determines the harvest. **Whatever is drummed into the minds of the children of any given generation will become the prevailing worldview of that society within only a few decades of time. Whoever controls the education of the children will control the destiny of that society. Case in point – Nazi Germany under Adolf Hitler. Secular humanists and atheists within the United States of America are raising up a generation that has been taught nothing of Christian values or the Christian influence on the Constitution or the Bill of Rights of the United States of America. A thought will lead to an action, that action repeated will lead to habit, that habit repeated will lead to a personal character, and the character of a person will lead directly to his or her destiny and it all starts with a thought or way of thinking.**

A "stream of consciousness" flows from the future, passes through the present, and moves into the realm of history, and it all happens in the blink of an eye. William James coined the term *stream of consciousness* in some of his writings (James, 1997, 307). The idea that our thoughts proceed upon our minds in some unpredictable fashion is not so far-fetched; being bombarded by thoughts is not an isolated experience. Many individuals speak of such things happening to them.

In conjunction with the idea of a "stream," some individuals have used the idea of a "field" (Lewin, 1997, 423) In this "field," ideas or meditations seem to just pop up out of nowhere into our consciousness from our subconscious. I suppose that would make the "field" or "plain"—as it may be thought of or visualized—the parchment or tapestry of our conscious mind. This mental parchment or tapestry is then written on with our immediate thoughts and abstract particles of thoughts, seeks other strands of thoughts from the past to link up with, and grabs hold of them in order to make a meaningful cognitive joining, make a subjective connection, or try to make meaning of the present experience.

I would suggest that our thoughts are not stand-alone items. They do not just materialize with no prerequisite expenditure of energy involved in their formulization. There are triggers to all our thought patterns. "Assimilate and accommodate" (Piaget, 1966) is suggested as an explanation for how we put particular thoughts in our minds (fields) or how we store them in some tributary upstream so that they may latch onto some familiar current heading downstream to our conscious mind—our intellect, the part of our consciousness that holds little self-talk conversations with our inner man (*man* as in gender-neutral mankind).

When we first come across an object in the physical realm, we have to find somewhere to store the image and information relating to it. We need a place to accommodate new information to which we have never been exposed. Think of it as putting a new file in your filing cabinet. You have other files in your filing cabinet, but no information similar to this new information. There are no "items of similarity," so you open up a whole new file to accommodate the data. If there had been "similar" items in other files, you would have naturally filed the new material with those of similar structure or concept.

In your mind (soul), there is a similar process going on each time you obtain information. If you have never seen anything like it, you start a "new" file to accommodate this new information. Well, you know, after awhile there is no really new information that doesn't somehow have things in common with what is in one or more files you've already accumulated. So instead of opening a new file, you simply put new information into an existing file that will "assimilate" it.

As you can see, when you get to be a few years old, you have pretty much run out of new stuff to accommodate, and you now mostly have to assimilate information into existing files. Of course, the basis for comparison of information is subjective to an individual's own understanding of circumstances, situations, and knowledge related to each item, whether it's a physical item or an intellectual concept that is being considered. When it comes to filing information, never forget that facts change but the truth always remains the same. An understanding of the truth and the correct application of it is wisdom. Erroneous "facts" that change over time often become erroneous assumptions that lead individuals into destructive behaviors.

Like a computer, our mind has many, many folders. Some have quite a bit of information in them, and some are not used all that often. They are files with only small bits of information stored in them—"memory traces" left by past experiences. These memory traces can simply be the emotional impact an event had without an actual storage of the experience itself. Yet these files can be triggered (opened) by something as silly as an odor or even a vaguely familiar environment; objects can trigger thoughts and emotions!

Isn't it fascinating how our minds and bodies work together? Sometimes an emotional response (our subconscious) can get to our bodies before the thought has even arrived in consciousness. Past emotional responses can be "tagged" to an actual event, and a similar event can light up a whole network of emotions even though the event is not consciously registering in the here and now. The body kicks into its fight-or-flight mode, synchronizing emotional distress with physical preparedness to meet any challenge, even if it is still unknown at that moment. The thought may be just starting to break ground in the "field" or only just beginning to dribble into the current upstream current, and the familiar emotional distress can bring on feelings of dread or fear.

As an adult, a person may have many phobias about certain, and perhaps multiple, events or objects. Sometimes we don't even remember that these events or fear of objects are even in some file in our mind. If an individual was beaten as a child with a belt in a particular room of the home, then either the room or the object—or similar places or objects—may evoke unpleasant responses. That scenario is just a simple example of how emotions can sometimes beat the buzzer to our consciousness, the "buzzer" being the hard-core memory. Every event of our past, including thoughts about those events and the emotions tagged to those events, is filed somewhere in our mind. It may not be in a "ready file" right up front in our mind; it may be way in the back, a little dusty or very dusty, having not been called on to assimilate any new material for a very long time, but it is there! A little girl's experience with the inappropriate behavior of a relative or long hours locked in a dark basement as the punishment for a child's mistake—they're there in the labyrinth of our mind. Some people refer to them as the skeletons in our closets. The scriptures call them strongholds that control and direct us, often without our permission. Sometimes we just give in because it is less painful than trying to delete the file. The more you give in out of anxiety and a fear of confrontation, the stronger the stronghold becomes. With each success in the manipulation of our behavior, the habitual response becomes stronger as a way to cope with the anxiety and fear gripping our hearts out of the darkness that still remains in our soul, mind, will, and emotions.

Pain in the familiarity of the everyday files

There are other files in our system that have different ways of controlling us through our response to their influences. A way of thinking is a lifestyle, a habitual design of influence. These files are the files that are always in use; there is no dust on them. They run the show. How we talk, how we dress, how we relate to others, the "mask of sanity" that we allow others to see when they confront us in life—these systems are roughly related in that they are the "operating systems" of our everyday lives.

All our strategies for acceptance and self-worth are woven together to structure our personalities in such a way as to give us significance and worth in this life. This process forms a "dynamic interrelated system" that controls all aspects of our physical and emotional behavior, and it is based on files that hold information that have been accumulated over a lifetime. Whether that life has been long or short makes no difference; all that is known is filed—right, wrong, or indifferent; behavioral experience and perceptions based on subjective defaults (guiding fictions) that rule the system of new information filing and the retrieval of all assimilated information.

Professionals call being raised in an environment with many "healthy" interactions as being raised in an enriched environment. This is a "leg up" when it comes to being able to cope with life events, such as schooling and then higher education, getting married and having a family, being a socially acceptable citizen of a society and doing your "duty" to stand for values that are expounded by the ideology of your culture. Those of us who are pure and morally motivated benefit society as a whole.

This means *direction* should be given to each individual as they grow older and experience life. If early experience dictates later behavior, society needs to be very careful regarding what the upcoming generation is taught is acceptable behavior within any given society. It is important because what is learned through experience and formal education for a generation will indeed be the law of the land in the next generation. There seems to be a conflict in today's society regarding what is "good" and "healthy" for an individual's mental concepts—an individual's worldview.

Because catalogues are organized into categories, most catalogue items can be found in an orderly arrangement. As you go through the catalogue, you will see that the items are categorized into specific sections depending on the type of item. This is very similar to the idea of assimilation by association, except when you get a catalogue it is complete in what the publisher wants to show you. Some people have their minds categorized like a catalogue, with no room for anything that is not already found in its pages. It is fixed and complete, and nothing new is added (assimilated). New information is examined in a cursory way but then discarded if it doesn't fit the paradigm (the prevailing fixed interrelated system of dynamic thought and concepts). This type of closed mindedness can be for good or evil depending on the precepts used to either accept or reject new concepts and old ideas.

It is a fact that how you raise a child (the next generation) will indeed influence how they think and perceive the world environment they live in. Secular ideologies based in godless concepts of humanism and relativism are the very seeds of destruction that are being sown in the secular ground of a dying evolutionary explanation for the existence of all things seen. It is a teaching that seeks to revert us back to a time when pagan beliefs were the fundamental understanding of both the seen and unseen world.

There are also many other spiritual explanations and gods to explain the seen world. A *Star Wars*, the-force-be-with-you explanation evolved from years of *Star Trek* Roddenberryian spiritualism, based in the unscientific view of extraterrestrial intelligence. It is a feel-good, anything-goes type of living predicated on the trinity of me, myself, and I. It is based on selfishness at the expense of anything or anybody else. Amoral is not a correct label because if there is no absolute morality, how can something be amoral? Paganism isn't godless, quite the contrary. It has a god for any and all things. It is as scattered and diverse as to be meaningless on any functional level beyond the individual. It leads to the destruction of an individual human entity.

In order to establish "sound" thinking and "sound" decision making, an individual needs a storehouse of sound information from which to draw on to evaluate and examine any given situation. It is imperative that this information isn't tainted by dysfunctional material from corrupted files that are somehow similar or have "trace experiences" that dilute the substance of the material value of the file into something distant and vaguely believable. In short, if the concept of a Creator got filed with Bugs Bunny and Mickey Mouse, there will be some difficulty in overcoming that person's reluctance to examine the inferential scientific evidence that so obviously points to an intelligence design concept of all that we observe in the cosmos.

Things not seen do not exist

Is there such a file in our minds left over from an earlier time in our lives? If we as children had assimilated into our minds the concept that all things not seen do not exist, we would have been in trouble when it came to expanding our minds by assimilating new theories of physics, mathematics, and the like. We already have accommodations for such thinking in our psyche. We simply need to assimilate the material into existing files. Right?

If the generations that are being raised up at this time don't hear anything but one concept of human existence and how it all came to be, what will they do with the idea of "creative design" (CD)? They will have no problem with evolutionary theory; they will just dump that into the force-be-with-you-file or the *Star Trek* file, whichever they choose to use. Secular societal forces have kept that nonsense alive for quite a few decades now. They can't seem to stop blowing up space shuttles, but they have the pupils believing in advanced extraterrestrial life-forms and space missions to space stations and beyond.

We have a whole upcoming generation that has, in large part, never heard the truth about creation. Or if they have heard the truth, the only file into which they have to assimilate it is the one with the tooth fairy and the Easter bunny and whatever wishful thinking geared for children they have accommodated somewhere in the files of their minds. There is most assuredly a Disney file titled "wish upon a star," as well as one for self-actualizing promises of the tenets of self-determination through positive thinking and trusting in an innate force for success in life. These past couple of generations have been taught to assimilate anything religious or in reference to a personal God into the file with the rabbits and the fairies, the file marked for ignorance and young children only. This idea has been reinforced by those who teach in public and private schools and also by those who write and publish news shows and newspapers and by radio and TV outlets across the nation. It is indeed a conspiracy. The conspirators are the true ignorant ones; they are the first wave of deceived minds raised up from the "don't talk about a God or Jesus" cohort group, who were raised in the occult of individual empowerment.

it is not as if they believe that this universe was created by design and want to hide the fact from everyone. They don't want to believe it at all, even when the evidence points directly to that fact. They are the crop that was harvested in the middle of the last century by intellectuals who hated God because of their preferences, not because of any scientific inference that He didn't exist. This "herd of independent thinkers" has managed to remove any place in the thinking of the next impressionable generation to even consider God and Jesus as anything more than a fairy-tale notion. With that notion is the notion that people of faith are the ones who are the cause of the global woes. Go to any college or university history class and you will hear how religion, patriotism, and nationalism have caused all wars since time began. All wars have also been promoted by the male gender, according to the writers of this new history, and this is giving rise to a new radical feminism.

These dysfunctional ideas are just concepts in the minds of confused secular men and women. We are told that these "unseen" concepts (e.g., religion, etc.) must be done away with. We need to be one big happy family. We all need to go to the United Nations and sing together and become one happy bunch with the same worldview à la John Lennon. This is the "programming" that is going on within the secular school systems of the United States of America at this very moment—a tearing down from within by a group of "utopianism" morons set on ideologies steeped in perverted concepts of freedom and liberty. This sludge is seeping in, not from the federal government as much as it is through education and foundations aiming to tear down the United States.

They want to have one world-governing body to bring us all some false utopia.

Some parents recently stated that they didn't want their children saying the pledge of alliance to the American flag in school because it was in conflict with their (the parents') worldview. Obviously these parents were very well indoctrinated into not only the secular idea of society, but now they don't even want to acknowledge the American society as the way to pursue liberty and justice for all. Their mental file banks have been corrupted by non-American doctrine put forth right here within our own country. The United States is being destroyed from within its own boundaries. It is not a freedom of speech issue; it is a treason issue and should be addressed as such. The forces that gather to destroy the American Constitution by perverting what it actually says about freedom should be taken to task in no uncertain terms.

Dysfunctional thinking simply doesn't function

If our national leaders have fallen into this secular trap, well then, so be it. If they continue to keep any concept of God out of public education through the perversion of the secular legislators, we as citizens need to pull our children out of the public school system. The fight over "vouchers" is more about what will be taught than about where it will be taught. If the conspirators lose the children of the next two generations, they lose it all. If they lose the opportunity to dictate what mental files will be allowed to have credibility in the next generation, they will have people of faith competing in the arena of ideas. They cannot allow people to have firm convictions on issues such as morality and the idea of an absolute truth and a sovereign country that professes these ideas to the rest of the world as a concept for living. They want to deny the right to autonomous living with a Christian influence with absolutely no regard for what is good for the society as a whole.

Repairing the damage, restoring sanity

Repairing the damage done by secularism in our educational system is going to be very difficult, if it can be done at all. It is not as if these poor moronic individuals are doing anything they don't wholeheartedly believe is true. They believe there is absolutely no personal Creator. These individuals do at some level buy into the pantheistic view of the-force-be-with-you kind of Eastern mysticism. There is no accountability with the old *Star Wars/Star Trek* philosophy of spiritualism. It is just Eastern religion repackaged for an I-want-to-feel-good society of already mentally deficient, educated individuals.

Many of these people were not always deficient in their epistemological functioning. They come from practicing Christian families, but they've been told that they must go to college to succeed in this society. Part of that intentional training is secularizing them. People wonder why children are going off to school and having the faith "beaten" out of them. It is intentional and paid for by tax dollars. If the professors don't finish the job, there is no need to worry. Students will be shamed into silence by the powers that control what the society is exposed to. Said powers will promote an overwhelmingly negative view of people who believe in a personal deity and His Son. Constant ridiculing and belittling is the theme of the day now and has been for over fifty years. They attack any idea put forth as a moral view that society needs to embrace in order to function and to carry on into the future the values that "build up" a society rather than the corrupt values that destroy society. Amoral people want amoral attitudes to prevail in government under the disguise of privacy and individual freedoms based on individual desires.

It is not as if the federal government doesn't make some attempt at keeping things under control, but it is the poor slobs who are making law from the bench with such poor, dysfunctional paradigms that are killing society. It is no accident. Look in your rearview mirror; legalizing drugs is closer then it appears. Sexual contact between adults and adolescents is right there also. They just have to get some judge to rule that the age requirement is unconstitutional because it violates a young person's right to privacy. I mean, if you don't need anyone's consent to terminate a life, why do you need consent to conceive it? If adolescents can "divorce" their parents because they don't like the rules of the house, who is to say with whom they can sleep and or with whom they can have a sexual relationship? Oh yeah, that will be some utopia. Get ready to apologize to Megan's Law's recipients. Now they don't have to hunt their prey. They can just use the old "take them out to dinner" gag.

There is a body of research that shows that having "religious faith" is one component in determining whether an adolescent will be involved with drugs, alcohol, and premarital sex. Saying premarital sex is wrong is almost laughable seeing as how some think we need to get rid of marriage altogether because it is an old-fashion institution. Sex education in the school system almost always involves what would have been considered pornography less than twenty years ago. I mean really, prophylactics and bananas in a third-grade class room? The inmates are running the asylum, and they're mostly on "feel-good" meds.

If you have no clue about what the normal use of a family is or what the normal use of children is or what the normal uses of your genitals are, then abuse is inevitable.

Abuse is abnormal use, and it is not relative to the situation. It is spelled out in law. The sad thing is that law is not like truth. Laws change to suit individual preferences when the people no longer speak through elected individuals but rather are dictated to through self-appointed kings who were suppose to be judges.

There are ways to stop this insanity, but people of faith with Christian values must stand up and make themselves heard before they die and America as our founding fathers thought of it dies with them.

Dust off your faith, and come home to God. Take a stand for virtue and honor before it is stolen right out from under your nose. Then it will be anything goes. If you are just a "religious" person, you might simply say, so what? Maybe it is time for no more of this morality stuff. You need to come home to God. You've been robbed mentally, and you've let the thief in through the front door of your eyes and ears. Your mind is smothered in filth. The filth has been laying around so long in your mind and heart that it actually has become the norm; it looks normal.

Sometimes these dysfunctional files in our minds are opened not by some horrific event that steals our faith. Sometimes they are opened with our permission, motivated by our own carnal desires. It doesn't matter how they became open, they are "strongholds" to be used by the enemy to tear us down and steal not only our futures but our children's and grandchildren's futures as well.

No one can argue that our experiences don't have some, if not a major, effect on our lives and our behavior—how we act, how we relate to others, how we relate to ourselves. Some individuals come from environments that are sterile and uninviting, if not downright hostile.

Some of us come from enriched environments, places where there were healthy interactions and words of encouragement to help us believe in ourselves and in the obvious reality of a Creator and His Son.

Each of these beliefs will bring about a whole different filing system in the minds of those involved. Where do the dredges of society come from? When you dredge, you drag the bottom to remove what is not wanted. The lower culture, the subculture, is a direct result of the wonderful new concepts of family, country, and God's Son Jesus Christ. Not all religions are the same, and not all religions lead to the same place. You ex-Christians who have been pulled away by your own desires better get back on that narrow path home while you still have some control over your own thinking. It won't be long, and soon your children will come home from college and steal your faith or what's left of it.

Your kids will come home from a place you thought was safe, and it will be like the body snatchers got them. They will look right through you and smile a condescending smile of tolerance. The government and the elected officials have let people of faith down. They are aliens in this land of our founding fathers. They are killing us from the inside out. It is like those 1960s' science fiction flicks that want to scare you at the end of some nonsense movie: only this time it is true.

Beware!
Watch and be alert!
The secular humanists are here.
Put them where they belong: in the circular file.

Chapter 3

A Healthy Worldview Is Not Subjective: Preferring Preference over Inference

There are so many so-called new concepts in cognitive and learning theories these days, such as the fact that when a person smiles, the muscle actions of his or her face cause more blood flow to the brain and more oxygen to be supplied to the cranial environment for utilization by the neurological network for optimum performance. Other concepts include: whistle a happy tune; there is nothing to fear or be apprehensive about except the concept of fear itself; fear anticipates negative consequences in regard to the individual; worry changes nothing—it confuses and distracts from positive strategies for resolutions; and worry cannot change circumstances, but positive thoughts can generate productive outcome strategies.

Dwelling on life circumstances can cause stress on the body and the mind; mediating on negative events can cause anxiety; and thinking about these events does nothing to change them. Prior to this century, these facts were all known to be true, but they were discarded and then reorganized within a scientific environment and declared to be a new revelation of scientific inquiry with all its statistical outcomes to prove it. I get the impression that sometimes when individuals find out a truth about behavior, they somehow think they really have accomplished something. Finding something that has always been there is simply attesting to the fact of its existence; it's not the same as creating it. And when something works and through trial and error proves to have a specific outcome, it need not be discarded simply because no one has figured out the "why" of it.

It seems it's all right to use a strategy for intervention in an area of mental illness if the "why" of the intervention's success is understood but not if the "why" can't be pinned down empirically by the scientific community. How else do you explain the blatant disregard within the scientific community of direct intervention techniques within Christian writings? Take for instance the following Bible passages:

- Luke 12:25: "Who of you by worrying can add a single hour to his life?" (NIV)
- Luke 12:26: "Since you cannot do this very little thing, why do you worry about the rest?" (NIV)
- Philippians 4:8: "And now, brothers, as I close this letter, let me say this one more thing: Fix your thoughts on what is true and good and right. Think about things that are pure and lovely, and dwell on the fine, good things in others. Think about all you can praise God for and be glad about." (TLB)

So when you tell someone not to exaggerate a situation or to stop dwelling on negative aspects of a given situation, that worrying about something is not going to change the situation but rather will cause physiological activities that can cause illness, it's a biblical concept. And telling someone to think positive is a biblical principle for good mental and physical health as well. It appears that we as a people have become so sophisticated that belief in the only real God is considered foolishness. We take the principles but deny the author. Well, that's covered in the Bible also. Romans 1:21 reads, "Yes, they knew about him all right, but they wouldn't admit it or worship him or even thank him for all his daily care. And after awhile they began to think up silly ideas of what God was like and what he wanted them to do. The result was that their foolish minds became dark and confused" (TLB). Romans 1:22 continues, "Claiming themselves to be wise without God, they became utter fools instead" (TLB).

There are truths that our society must come to realize, just as our founding fathers understood there are absolutes within which a society must function to survive. The shame of it is that they couldn't fathom a Christian community would ever be so lax in its duty to pass down these truths or that a secular, Christian-hating, elitist group would somehow gain control of the government and use a perverted interpretation of the Constitution to try to box Christian morals and authority into a small corner of society to the extent that an entire generation could be raised with no moral values or understanding of the reality of God in an individual's life. And now these debased individuals are getting elected into bureaucratic office by other dissolute citizens.

You know, education is no indication of character any more than athletic ability is. We have developed a generation that is lost and confused. They're self-serving, and many are antisocial. They have no hope for the future. They view destruction in almost every aspect of their daily lives, and we wonder why they act in such a manner that society would call them abnormal. The lack of moral absolutes under the heading of "freedom" is laughable. No one has the right to do what is wrong! Which of course begs the question, who will decide what is lawful and what is unlawful? What promotes well-being within a society, and what causes the inhabitants of a society to become destructive to themselves and those around them? This has nothing to do with *America* or *democracy* or political theories of government. This has to do with what is acceptable in the sight of civilization as a whole, regardless of political establishment. What allows people to live mentally and physically healthy lives?

What are laws anyway? There would be no laws if there were no lawbreakers. Laws are made only for lawbreakers. If an individual knows he shouldn't steal from others and he doesn't, then the laws about theft don't apply to that individual. If you don't break the law, you have no guilt or apprehension regarding that law. Christian restrictions on human behavior don't cause guilt and shame; it is thinking that causes people to experience distress.

People experience distress when they do something there may be no law against, yet they feel guilt. The laws against adultery have become unenforceable these days, but most individuals feel guilt about committing adultery, not because of the concept of law but rather because of the inert feelings of spiritual betrayal. Those who don't feel as if they have betrayed a fundamental obligation of commitment to another living human being have had their hearts and minds seared shut by the false teachings of secular humanism: if it feels good, do it. Adultery is destructive within any relationship between a man and a woman, even without the law against it. It's unacceptable behavior within a society because it damages families and society as a whole.

People generally laugh when someone uses the word sin. Sin is a joke to society; it's considered a religious concept with no basis in a free society. In fact, you could simply change the word "sin" to the phrase "behavior conducive to destruction within an emotional or physical framework." Don't sleep with your neighbor's wife; it could cost you your life. Lay off alcohol in your life; alcohol leads to destruction. Both of these religious concepts are right and seem to be proving themselves in our society today. Does alcoholism cause mental problems for people? Can its present-day counterpart, drugs, play a part in the mental illness prevalent in today's society? Of course it does. Who could argue intelligently otherwise? What does the Bible say about alcoholism, or for that matter any addiction that alters an individual's thinking (e.g., drugs)?

Proverbs 23:29 reads, "Whose heart is filled with anguish and sorrow? Who is always fighting and quarreling? Who is the man with bloodshot eyes and many wounds? It is the one who spends long hours in the taverns, trying out new mixtures" (TLB).

Christian truth is an adequate intervention for the professional field that deals with people who are confused and lost within the pressures of unrestrained, self-seeking societal living. Why are people so afraid of Christian concepts? They are afraid that they might have to live up to and according to concepts that enhance society as a whole, without regard to the lust of the individual.

The Ten Commandments should become a tool for instruction to cut off the mental confusion that individuals experience within themselves—confusion about what promotes well-being and a healthy lifestyle. Alas, the whole concept is lost on a secular world that wants to accumulate everything and fornicate with anything or anybody. This secular world is full of social deviants gathering in their little in-groups, hating the out-groups, demanding no limitations on their behavior under the pretext of freedom, and the demanding medication to get them through the day. Boy, that's freedom all right. There are things that our bodies will do physiologically if we don't, through the intervention of language and thought woven together in our minds, come to a conclusion of sense toward our fleshly existence. Who is going to be in charge? Who is going to follow who? Will our intellect allow our physiological responses to control our behavior, or will our minds intervene to control the biochemical reactions that emanate from an otherwise healthy mind?

There are things that we as humans just naturally want to do when we allow the same nature that controls animals to reign supreme within our beings with no restraint based in moral and societal values. But of course, common sense even hinted at in "Christian" principle can't be allowed into the public arena, which has been set up by self-serving politicians under the excuse of separation of church and state—a concept that doesn't exist in our Constitution. When does Christian principle state ever so clearly about the unrestrained human nature?

I advise you to obey only the Holy Spirit's instructions. He will tell you where to go and what to do, and then you won't always be doing the wrong things your evil nature wants you to do. We naturally love to do evil things that are just the opposite from the things that the Holy Spirit tells us to do; and the good things we want to do when the Spirit has His way with us are just the opposite of our natural desires. These two forces within us are constantly fighting each other to win control over us, and our wishes are never free from their pressures. When you are guided by the Holy Spirit, you need no longer force yourself to obey Jewish laws. But when you follow your own wrong inclinations, your life will produce evil results: impure thoughts, eagerness for lustful pleasure, idolatry, spiritism (that is, encouraging the activity of demons), hatred and fighting, jealousy and anger, constant effort to get the best for yourself, complaints and criticisms, the feeling that everyone else is wrong except those in your own little group. And there will be wrong doctrine, envy, murder, drunkenness, wild parties, and all sorts of those things. Let me tell you again as I have before: anyone living that sort of life will not inherit the Kingdom of God (Gal. 5:16–21 TLB).

By definition, the Kingdom of God is where peace of mind is acquired—a oneness with peace and joy and the things that bring true pleasure to an individual's life. Romans 14:17 reads, "For the kingdom of God is not a matter of eating and drinking, but of righteousness, peace and joy in the Holy Spirit" (NIV). These are the interventions that need to be cognitively taught all over again to a generation that is dying in its own confusion. Once integrated into the life of an individual as a lifestyle, it can be passed down to the next generation. It will be learned by the children of Christian parents simply by being in the presence of such behavior and attitudes.

Now I understand that all Christians are not perfect, but neither are the ones that make mistakes—hypocrites. A hypocrite is an intentional pretender. Hypocrites are out there all right, but not in the quantity that the world would like people to believe. The world sneers and mocks only because it is afraid someone might listen to people of faith, who not only talk the talk but also walk the walk and have victory in their lives.

There are those who demand their own little perversions be given the same respect as what is healthy and good. They do so under the excuse of social prejudice against alternative behavior, which they claim is their right of self-expression. When individuals find themselves having difficulty in their thoughts—which leads to stress, anxiety, and depression or a combination of all three in different degrees—all the vain excuses to justify their position actually hides the causes for any or all of them from view; it is the behavior itself that generates the outcome, not the opinions of others. If one commits murder it is not the fact that others think murder is wrong that causes the guilt and remorse of the one who committed the act. It is the act itself—which is hideous—that brings on the cognitive distress experienced. It is the same with adultery; it is betraying one's own self.

Cognitive intervention seems to be on the right track for most of the problem. It's called "stinkin' thinkin'," or more scientifically, "erroneous beliefs." Erroneous beliefs on the part of so-called highly educated individuals are still wrong concepts based in fallacious paradigms with no foundation other than false hypotheses paraded to the lay person as factual information. Their worse scenarios are based on doomsday theories that alter governmental policy regarding individual freedoms. Many of our leaders have become delusional in their thinking, and as stated, a delusion can have the force of reality when it is the basis for physical decisions and policies.

Delusions are just as destructive within a governmental body as they are for a mentally unstable individual; a collective lunacy is still lunacy. Does it not trouble anyone that the world body is actually considering a strategy for blowing up asteroids that might be headed toward Earth sometime in the future? This is a government policy based on Hollywood and geological fantasy—a world deceived into making absurd policies aimed at governing the populous of not only this country but also trying to get the global community to come together in regard to erroneous environmental issues that would subvert the sovereignty of the Untied States of America under the guise of global cooperation. If the individuals who make these policies are not delusional, they seem to be intentionally subversive. It is similar to how Hitler's Germany intended to use the lawful exercise of governmental infiltration to perpetuate what seemed to be lawful sedition on the part of elected global radicals, whose doctrine was a one-world government that would dictate to all nations over and above the sovereignty of any given country. The United Nations is a joke that can kill, and the National Education Association (NEA) is the vehicle to indoctrinate a compliant generation. Not all mental illness is obvious to others. Some mental illnesses come disguised and promoted as intellectual genius.

Demons and devils can be understood by a lay person who may entertain an air of archaic beliefs, but in reality the concepts of devils and demons describe the influence of the perverted intellectual thinking of a generation of leaders whose foundational thinking is nothing more than educated perversions of truth. And they indeed come to kill, steal, and destroy the freedom that was once ours under not only the Constitution of the United States but as God-given rights to the entire human race. The humanists, in their ignorance, run around singing the praises of the very forces that will take captive not only their minds but also their children's minds. I'll leave you with a warning from over nineteen centuries ago. You can call it religious rhetoric in a pluralistic society that thinks all concepts are equal, or you can wake up and come to yourself and realize you are indeed being duped by your own so-called enlightenment and vain thinking. Stop listening to the world's "Hollywood" scripts for survival, and see if in your own capacity you might actually have a unique individual thought based on the reality around you. If a pseudointellectual should actually have this thought, let us pray it doesn't die a slow death of loneliness.

> *"See to it that no one carries you off as spoil or makes you yourselves captive by his so-called philosophy and intellectualism and vain*

deceit (idle fancies and plain nonsense), following human tradition (men's ideas of the material rather than the spiritual world), just crude notions following the rudimentary and elemental teachings of the universe and disregarding [the teachings of] Christ (the Messiah)" (Col. 2:8 KJV).

"Christianity is not a religion—it's a relationship!" (Luke 15:24 The Message).

Chapter 4

Who Is a Hypocrite? Isolated Strongholds

Behavior generates outcomes in epistemological reality

So what can we say about all this? Paradigms, paradigms, the foundations of an array of human thinking, some seemingly based in the facts of material existence, others merely systematic conjectures of the human mind following so-called logical syllogisms. The intellectual geniuses of our generation look down on the ignorant as if they are children who need to be led into the promised land of a utopian existence by the renaissance boys of the new environmental global concerns of a world community waiting for the answers about the suffering of the world masses. Democracy, socialism, human rights, animal rights—since the turn of the century, everybody seems to have an answer to the problem. Many themes have been tried, only to be proven to be fallacies of false hope by their inability to change anything. Everybody is a genius in the last half of the last decade of the twentieth century.

When I was fifty-three years old and sitting among young people in an institution of higher learning, I gleaned the knowledge my peers have accumulated over a lifetime of learning, professors from a cohort group that began its existence after the completion of the first half of this enlightened century. These free thinkers equate fundamental material knowledge with intelligence. But finding out about something that always existed is not intelligence or the creation of something new; it's simply the exercise of the human intellect to the point of understanding what has always been. It is not really a great achievement when one considers how long it has taken humanity to understand what has been right before its eyes for really quite a long time now. The inquisitive mind, the searching personality, and the hope of bettering our own existence have proved to be quite strong motivators in the process we call "scientific research."

Scientific research is the search for things that can be proven in the sight of men so that others can build upon these facts with confidence of a firm foundation for experimentation; search for the way things work together in this material reality. It seems everything can be put in its proper place except for the human element. People are different; each individual is unique in his or her ability to be totally different from one another. All the working parts are relatively the same, and the systems that control the energy of life are the same in each human. The anatomy and the physical processes that keep us "alive" are the same, but the essence of each and every one of us is different.

A huge bundle of chemical reactions and electrical output control this flesh we call our bodies. *Our bodies*—what a simple statement for a complex creation. I wouldn't get into the paradigms of thinking that on one hand says we have become what we are over millions of years of step-by-step trial and error and the other hand seems to think our genetic makeup came from visitors from another planet who bred within the human-animal population of this third rock from the sun and will be back to solve all our problems. One explanation is as ignorant as the other.

Worldview engineering

The first explanation has us putting animals and the environment on a pedestal, as if we are the aberrant life-form on this planet. We, the human race, are the dysfunctional intellectual life, the destroyer of all that is good and "natural." The second explanation tells us that we are nothing more than genetically altered apes, waiting for our genetic biological cousins to come and rescue what they left behind on their travels through the stars. This generation has watched far too many episodes of *Star Trek* over the years. Do you honestly think these shows that penetrate our domiciles are there by accident? Or is it possible that they are there to train up a generation toward a fundamental paradigm regarding the whole scope of their thinking?

I have to laugh sometimes when I realize the truth of what a professor at my university stated in class during a lecture one day. The only reason the *show* is being broadcast is to gain the attention of an audience so that an advertiser can sell a product to make money for the executives, employees, and stockholders of the company of the advertised product; for no other reason does this *entertainment* exist. I found that to be a pretty enlightening statement. Now the rest of the world may have already known that and I in my ignorance was alone enlightened, but I don't think that I was the only person who wasn't consciously aware of that fact. That would explain why there is such a correlation to the filth we find on the glowing pulpit of the world today. The sponsors will support any type of depravity as long as it sells product to an audience. Some shows appeal to our lowest base nature and no one seems to notice or care what it is doing to the thinking of the viewing public.

Shows have become demeaning, profane, violent, perverted, and generally trash. It's because the shows reflect what the people who watch them are like in their little chemical minds. If nobody is watching, nobody is sponsoring. There is an exception to that statement. A particular group could fund a show, whether it be a network that has its own social agenda or monies used to support a social brainwashing of a *brain-dead* public to accept the premise that freedom is the absence of restraints of any kind within the socialization of its members. The show and the group sponsoring it push the idea that anything is acceptable if (1) the participants are "adults" and if (2) those participating are "willing" and doing so from a position of "free" choice. This, by the way, is a slow cancer within any society. This paradigm of thinking corrodes the foundation of society and, over time, it will cause the whole house to come crashing down.

A purposeful plan of destruction

There are, of course, those who may think that if society (as we know it traditionally in America) came crashing down, it would be a good thing. If the powers that be—those mean old money grabbers and abusers of the simple people—could have their system of control destroyed, we would all be better off. We could go back to living in harmony with "Mother" nature. This particular group of fruitcakes has gained a considerable amount of strength over the past half century. That is not to deny the imperative that we all (as human beings) need to exercise good stewardship in relationship to our world and those things that coexist with us to maintain our physical lives. No one could logically support any premise that would destroy the things that make life possible on this unique sphere we all occupy.

I would wholeheartedly agree with the premise of good stewardship, but not with aberration of thought that puts "nature" above the free exercise of life of autonomous individuals. Don't you ever wonder why certain groups of individuals support the murder of large groups of people in third world countries? Why is there always the outcry against this type of behavior under the guise of genocide and yet the world community can never seem to get together to remove the anti-world, social personalities who do these things? Margaret Sanger would be able to tell you why: because it's a good idea to get rid of useless eaters.

It was the same reason immigrants to the United States of America at the turn of the century were refused entry into this country; those individuals were genetically inferior, and their breeding should have been controlled in order to purge this inferior element from the earth. If they can't legally be sterilized, they should be taught that as a socially depressed class of individuals they should not be forced to be population factories bound by offspring, depriving them of their exercise of autonomous equality. I mean after all, isn't it obvious that the world will become overpopulated? Then we will all starve, and the environment will be destroyed by a relentless effort to supply housing, food, and other resources to more and more of humankind.

The idea is to get people brainwashed into accepting the premise that eliminating the population on both ends of the spectrum would be best for all of us in the long run. The idea would be to control how many more biological units enter this realm and hasten the departure of those at the far end who have become nonproductive and just sit around enjoying accumulated material assets that could be better spent on those who are yet to come. I don't think it is the duty of the older citizens to get out of the way of the young. Human beings are not a kind of animal. They are totally different in their makeup; they are made in the image of their Creator. They are spiritual beings living in human bodies. They are human from conception, not potential humans but rather humans with potential and should be allowed to die a natural unassisted death.

Erroneous worldviews waste resources

Is the premise that the earth is one big living unit and we as humans are just a part of this living unit? That all humanity is in lockstep for the advancement of space exploration to the far beyond where utopia waits for future generations? Can anybody explain why in the vain imaginations of a whole generation of so-called intellectual beings, we as a people are complaining about the conditions within our society and yet are spending billions of dollars to float around the planet in sophisticated tin cans?

Those who want appropriations for such exploration will give you all the reasons you can imagine. These reasons are mostly built on false premises, but again the explanation is that future generations need to be thought of if the human race is to continue on when planet Earth dies because of overpopulation and bad stewardship of its resources. Who are these people? Sci-fi brainwashed idiots. Doesn't anybody realize that *Star Trek* is a fantasy? The statement that mankind can accomplish whatever it puts its mind to is quite true. But who decides what mankind puts its mind to anyway? Is it the sponsors of certain paradigms of thought who have the cash to inundate the thinking of the ignorant masses? Or do those who create such expressions of personal opinions based in their own debased nature keep pushing for the uninformed compliance of the general public in hopes of a greater fulfillment of the human race? Is it a single focus toward some unseen hypothesized destiny? What is it that people use in their lives to ground themselves to a solid foundation to get a grasp on a reality, some make-believe television show that seeks to bend their minds to a worldview of some contrived utopia? I would put to you that some people don't know what they believe and there are those who don't care what they believe as long as they *DON'T BELIEVE IN JESUS CHRIST As The Creator God.*

What a bunch of nonsense. The renaissance boys are going to demand obedience to the bigger ideal, the greater good. They will corrupt the best system of government ever devised in the history of mankind (one that is run/based on honor and principles of justice and duty) for the fulfillment of the life of an individual in conjunction with responsibility to the whole based on standards of morality and service toward others. Without the forced compliance to the fantasies of governmental programs based on prime-time episodes of the imaginations of moronic creators of delusions of intellectual prowess posing as scientific fact, lawmakers, judges, and the elite would be less able to directly influence the populace.

We become what we consume

A mutual admiration society—through the ability to sell products from unconcerned money men—has given socially inept, twisted, anti-morality, chemically altered geniuses the money and influence to befuddle the masses as people sit, basking in the blue glow of social engineering, with one hand in a bag and the other wrapped around a can. And our leaders are stymied to do anything about it because there is no scientific proof that viewing violence causes individuals to be violent. How did we get so stupid? How did these morons get in charge? Freedom does not mean no restraint from common sense. But you're imposing your will on others, they say, and therefore others can no longer be free to express themselves. It's a violation of their right to free speech and free expression, they say. I would put to you that no one has a right to express deviant amoral concepts that influence the minds of the masses into compliance between a sales pitch for nutritional cereal and a commercial for fermented hops.

I guess the obvious question that is always asked is who "has the right" to call one person's behavior more acceptable than that of another? Just a few years ago, a U.S. senator made an ignorant mistake; he called the United States a *Christian country*, and all the so-called intellectuals had a fit. It seems that they had evolved beyond such ridiculous epistemological paradigms as religious concepts; now they are waiting for spacemen to contact us. Now that's a real step up. They really ought to get their heads out from under botanical influences.

I would put forth the statement that President George Washington stated in his farewell speech. "Citizens, by birth or choice, of a common country, that country has a right to concentrate your affections. The name of American, which belongs to you in your national capacity, must always exalt the just pride of patriotism more than any appellation derived from local discriminations. With slight shades of difference, you have the same religion, manners, habits, and political principles. You have in a common cause fought and triumphed together; the independence and liberty you possess are the work of joint counsels, and joint efforts of common dangers, sufferings, and successes" (Washington, 1796) Does anyone really think that the common religion he refers to includes Eastern religions and witchcraft?

The zeitgeist (spirit) of the times

My professor noticed a conflict in this regard. He said, "Isn't it strange that such a statement could be made in the presence of a socially accepted paradigm of slavery and adultery?" I assume the adultery part referred to the inbreeding of slave owners with their female slaves—a common practice of "herd" expansion for the time period.

On the surface, this sounds like a statement that should be considered a contradiction. But if you were to read the accounts of a great American by the name of Frederick Douglass, you would get a perception of why and how this could happen in a Christian community. Slavery was a disease to both the white and the black, morally destroying both races. It was a deep-rooted paradigm that had become accepted as acceptable thinking for hundreds of years, and this thinking destroyed all who accepted it and clung to it as some sort of truth of existence.

Douglass describes his treatment in his master's household as he moved from the Deep South to more "civilized" parts (because of the exposure of slavery's expression to non-slaveholders) in the nearby northern states. This first meeting with a white Christian woman, the wife of a slave holder in Baltimore, proved to be enlightening to him in his understanding of the destructive power of slavery to all concerned.

I lived in Mater Hugh's family about seven years. During this time, I succeeded in learning to read and write. In accomplishing this, I was compelled to resort to various stratagems. I had no regular teacher. My mistress, who had kindly commenced to

> *instruct me, had, in compliance with the advice and direction of her husband, not only ceased to instruct, but had set her face against my being instructed by any one else. It is due, however, to my mistress to say of her, that she did not adopt this course of treatment immediately. She at first lacked the depravity, indispensable to shutting me up in mental darkness. It was at least necessary for her to have some training in the exercise of irresponsible power, to make her equal to the task of treating me as though I were a brute. My mistress was, as I have said, a kind and tender-hearted woman; and in the simplicity of her soul she commenced, when I first went to live with her, to treat me as she supposed one human being ought to treat another. In entering upon the duties of a slaveholder, she did not seem to perceive that I sustained to her the relation of a mere chattel, and that for her to treat me as a human being was not only wrong, but dangerously so. Slavery proved as injurious to her as it did to me. When I went there, she was a pious, warm, and tender-hearted woman. There was no sorrow or suffering for which she had not a tear. She had bread for the hungry, clothes for the naked, and comfort for every mourner that came within her reach. Under its influence, the tender heart became stone, and the lamblike disposition gave way to one of tiger-like fierceness. The first step in her downward course was in her ceasing to instruct me. She now commended to practice her husband's precepts. She finally became even more violent in her opposition than her husband himself. She was not satisfied with simply doing as well as he had commanded; she seemed anxious to be better. Nothing seemed to make her more angry than to see me with a newspaper. … that education and slavery were incomparable with each other (Douglass, 1845)*

To say that this behavior on the part of all slaveholders is a testimony to some kind of hypocrisy is incorrect. This lady simply went away from what Douglass himself describes as "pious and kind-hearted person," which was the exercise of her Christianity, because it was perverted by the paradigms of the present socially accepted behavior. It was the paradigm of society that perverted the truth of her religious faith.

The woman's bending her faith to society rather than insisting society bend to the truth of her Christian faith is not unlike today. Religious principle is mocked as hypocritical in today's society. It is not hypocritical, but like the woman Frederick Douglas describes, Christians of today are no different; they've bent their faith to conform to the socially acceptable thinking of the day, and it is to their own destruction. Religious thinking has been conformed in many cases to the brainwashing of compliance to the social climate. When individuals stand up for what is "true" and right, they are labeled the "radical right" by the intellectual conformists of the day. I'm sure if this woman described by Douglass had taken a stand for the moral ground and sought to organize others in opposition to the "social" thinking of the day, she would have suffered legal consequences. It is similar today as laws are being made and enforced to curb people's moral outrage regarding the filth that is paraded before the public as though it were normal, right, and acceptable.

Those who take a stand against amoral attitudes and behavior today are called bigoted and biased. Good has become evil, and those who stand for what has shown itself to be right are now portrayed as evil. Is pornography really a right when it has shown itself to be a strong correlate to sexual abuse and deviant behavior? Is abortion a right in view of a desire to save the world from overpopulation? The United States government is pushing for "family planning" or so-called "women's health care" throughout the world. Killing unborn children on the altar of this present environmental paradigm of overpopulation is as great an evil that is infecting the populous as much as slavery affected the South in the 1800s. Today we ask how they could have allowed it to happen ... Well, that question will be asked again, this time about this present-day society of death at both ends of the life cycle, about this society that advocates perversion and amoral behavior as the norm and looks at opposing viewpoints that demand this poisoning of our society be stopped as the ravings of some ignorant religious minority.

The media puts forth mindless supposition as the truth without any opposing viewpoint. The so-called educational television programs are nothing more than indoctrination of the fallacies of the intellectual fantasies of those who push their agendas into the minds of unsuspecting viewing audiences. I just learned last evening that a prehistoric fish that predates the dinosaurs is our earliest ancestor because it had bones that resemble fingers in its pelvic girdle area that happened to be the same size as a present-day man's. Why is it that I can see a vast audience sitting in their homes, nodding their heads in unison? I remember being taught in elementary school in the 1950s that we were all descendants of the animal kingdom. Pictured above the blackboard was a progression of knuckle-dragging species who eventually wore suits and carried briefcases—our evolutionary heritage expressed as fact. We were descendants of the caveman of Europe, who evolved from earlier primates; that is how it was put and with absolute certainty.

Now we hear that with the DNA testing of today, it has been found that the Neanderthals aren't even distant cousins to humans, just similarly designed; much like the chimpanzee, they are not related to human beings. As much as atheistic science tries, they can't find the source of humanity on the evolutionary tree. But that's not expressed on our wonderfully socially directed shows, which rewrite science to state in unsupported hypothesis—whatever benefits the predominate social thinking of the day—and state these erroneous conclusions as undisputed facts while only wishing and hoping they can find their *missing link.*

It is a sad state of affairs that we find ourselves in today. Children are shooting down children in school yards. Young mothers are strangling newborn babies in public bathrooms and then throwing them into trash cans. Why should a young woman be tried on a murder charge? If she had gone to a "women's health" professional, that "professional" could have merely almost delivered the baby and before total separation from the womb, sucked its brains out. He could have thrown it in the garbage and collected a government-subsidized payment for doing so. That sounds like population control paid for by our leaders in the paradigm of death in the name of population control. But the end doesn't justify the means, no matter how noble the perpetrators think their motives are.

I'll stand by what an unbiased thinker would conclude: morals and absolutes are not relative to time and space. They are timeless and unchanging, and it doesn't matter if the entire population joins hands and declares differently. The whole of the South declared slavery justified. They said Negroes were not humans and claimed they were the property of their owners. Now the same logic is being used in regard to a woman being the proprietor of her body and the life within it; it's her property and no one has the right to tell her she has to jeopardize her career and future by being encumbered by this biological pre-human fishlike creature. Well, I don't want to get sidetracked with issues that are so very clearly the Dred Scott decision of the 1960s, passed in the name of social pressure.

Seeking an answer

After returning to a university myself after an absence of many years from structured "higher learning" (there were training programs in the military and, of course, in my business adventures), I found that I had acquired a purposeful meaning for my time and energy: trying to help others through the difficulties of aberrant behavior generated by erroneous thinking or indeed bad behavior through observation and acclimation to dysfunctional strategies for living. The training I was attempting to obtain at the time would afford me the knowledge to identify such behavior in its many forms. Whether the dysfunction is causing distress in an individual or is simply revealing identifiers should allow me to help those who haven't yet come to distress but are either anxious or depressed with their present existence (the events in their everyday lives).

By definition, psychology is the study of and the attempt to explain psychological phenomena in terms of their biological foundations. In short, according to the *New Merriam-Webster Dictionary*, it is "the science of mind and behavior; the mental and behavioral characteristics of an individual or group." (*The New Merriam-Webster Dictionary*, 1989, G.K. Hall & Co.). Psychologists are individuals who have attempted to obtain a degree of understanding regarding why individuals and groups of individuals act and think the way they do. Psychologists can also identify behavior that may signal that a person harbors abnormal beliefs or delusional ideas that are related to conditions of mental abnormality. Then they can hypothesize why people find themselves in these conditions and run experimental tests to try to pinpoint common threads of evidence in the lives of these individuals that may account for their thinking, actions, lifestyles, and foundational belief systems that are unacceptable either to them or to those around them (e.g., physical violence).

Many individuals know when they are acting in a manner that is—outside their closer circle of friends—wrong or unacceptable by the standards set within their social environment. Police, ministers, and psychologists all receive the same uneasy stares from strangers around them when they state their occupations in a mixed social setting. It seems people perceive these groups to know what "lawful" behavior is and thus assume members of those groups can easily pick up on the simplest examples of behavior that could lead them to think an individual is not a law-abiding citizen. No normal individual wants to be thought of as unsocialized.

People who have made "law enforcement" their life's work tend to socialize with others in the same field. Cops hangout with cops and no one would say that *all* police officers are choir boys, but in today's environment of police work, the individual being considered is much more highly educated prior to police training. A background in college-level pre-law training, a moderate psychology background, and people skills are a must for the person looking to enter into police work, even at the local level. The police officer is trained to look for indicators in behavior that may signal a person's uneasiness in a given situation; thus, they make others uncomfortable. People do indeed know right from wrong and are guarded in their actions and speech around others whom they suppose are there to enforce the "law."

Ministers have the same problem in the presence of others who are not necessarily "morally" devoted in their choice of language in conversation or in their expressions of what they consider socially acceptable behavior based simply on their supposed freedom to do whatever they feel like doing at any given moment, without regard to the idea that something might be "socially" wrong.

To make this point, all you have to do is invite a priest to a cocktail party. The conversation becomes less vivid in its adjectives of expression, people tend to become less obviously intoxicated, and, amazingly, people don't usually like to smoke in the presence of a priest. Women who are generally flirtatious in their low-cut dresses suddenly begin to look for a shawl, and they become more aware of their body language. One has to wonder why this happens. Though many people and the media love to talk about a "man of God" doing something wrong in the eyes of the law, it makes you wonder why they take such glee in the mistakes of these individuals. Maybe in some perverted way they think it somehow justifies the behavior that they know is wrong in their own lives; it's the old attitude that "I may be bad but I'm not as bad as that hypocrite," a kind of justification in which we compare ourselves to the weakest, thus giving our self-esteem a hike up a notch or two and dumbing down our own morals.

Prisoners have made an art of comparisons. It seems everybody in jail is cool. Murders, rapist, robbers—they all fit into their little social classes, and at the bottom is the child molester. He is the social outcast, the leper. It's the idea that yes, we've been bad, but we're not as bad as that guy. When prisoners are brought before an individual for an examination of the things that have caused them to act and think in a particular manner, they get very guarded, almost as though revealing information about their lives and habits might actually give someone an edge in their treatment. They are fearful it might actually give someone the means by which to suggest strategies to help change their lifestyle of abhorrent behavior. This makes them nervous, as if changing their behavior will somehow change them into a socialized zombie of sorts. Someone who follows the rules is perceived as weak minded.

Prisoners know that they are lawbreakers. In many cases, that was the idea in the first place. They weighed the options and went for it, figuring the possibility of punishment was worth the reward of the moment, but they lost the game and got the punishment. What about people who break laws that are simply inertly known, laws that if you break them, you don't go to jail? But maybe you'll judge yourself guilty. How do you sentence yourself on such a charge? Are the criteria for the verdict sound? Was it imposed in your mind by social conditioning? Is it just some arbitrary code of conduct that need not be observed if you simply don't want to comply? Or are some behaviors just wrong within the human condition?

Who can explain the reasons an individual might experience feelings that interfere with his or her happiness or effectiveness in his or her everyday lives? Perhaps the study of and the attempt to explain psychological phenomena in terms of their biological foundations can give us some insight. Why is the mind influenced by what our bodies do, and how can an amoral mind lead to unacceptable behavior? Does erroneous thinking lead to erroneous actions? Do we act erroneously and then pay with guilt and shame after we figure out that our biological actions went beyond what we actually consider moral?

Words that have a strong concordance with the term *moral* within our society are words like *ethical*, *principled*, *proper*, *pure*, and *virtuous*.

Are we taught behaviors that would fall into these categories, or are some of them just simply such truisms of our human nature that acquiring them is not the problem? Rather the problem for certain individuals is overcoming them, and when they can't, they suffer. There is a thinking today that these codes of moral conduct are the source of stress and anxiety in our lives and that they need to be discarded as archaic philosophies that only damage our free will and expressions. Some argue that if it wasn't for morals, there would be a lot less people suffering from "mental" problems brought on by guilt and shame.

When someone says in a social conversation, "I'm a psychologist," all eyes sneak a peek, and then the conversation becomes guarded in the presence of the one who is perceived as "watching" for the signs of behavior that reveal inner thoughts and beliefs. People don't like it when they think someone else really might know what they're truly thinking or what they truly believe in their hearts and minds. Does anyone really want what they really are thinking broadcast to someone else? That's a delusion that schizophrenics have major problems dealing with. Is a psychologist really able to make determinations of that sort, to make a judgment of what is normal behavior and abnormal behavior? What are the criteria? The criteria are whether a person's thinking and actions have positive or negative effects on his or her personal lives.

A psychologist is attuned to "behavior" that may signal the real inner condition of an individual and not simply the "mask" we all wear when in contact with others. They are looking for the clues to the real you! They are the detectives of the expressions of human actions and subtle behaviors that broadcast what is really going on behind those "baby blues." And when distress is found, can they really help? Do they really have the answers? And if the answer to that question is yes, where did they get the answers?

Psychology is indeed a science. It has all its little tests to show outcomes of research procedures and intervention techniques on groups of individuals. Psychologists are always looking for the "proof" of what makes people act the way they do in particular patterns of behaviors. People were taught that way, they think that way, or they are chemically programmed that way. These are all interesting choices with many overlapping possibilities, many constellations of combinations that simply baffle the imagination. So many theories with so little conclusive evidence!

Thoughts—labyrinths of chemically produced electrical charges shooting through a maze of passageways controlling involuntary physical movement and purposeful directed movement that is first preceded by a "thought." What is a thought? Where does it come from? Does the thought come first and then the array of chemical actions manifests it into a physical action? Is it tangible or simply riding on the back of electrical energy that generates movement, pushing the charge through all the correct circuitry to accomplish its goals like the master of this fleshly machine we call home? Are we what we see in the mirror, or is who we are hidden somewhere at the control panel of electrical currents and chemical reactions pulling the switches on a less-than-perfect neurological control system and hoping for the best?

It all sounds a little philosophical. I guess it should. It was meant to. We will never prove as fact what we can't observe in the abstract. We will never see the night rider of our soul (intellect), only the footprints of his existence in the simplest of smiles or in the frowns of despair. Are there strategies of "controlled" thinking that we can use to influence his recklessness? And if he is us, then who is trying to get through to him? If he is our soul (intellect), then who is in there with him? And if he is a renegade, how can we strengthen the other enough to force this maverick into compliance with our will? Can our will be strength enough to control our actions? Can our will control the biochemical events that produce the actions that cause us to experience the emotional feelings of joy and despair, the distance between happiness and pleasure, and can sadness and emotional pain may simply be a thought away? No! Psychology is not as simple as mind over matter; it's more a matter of truth over confusion, a selection over individual direction, a conscious choice. Are there principles of truth (effectively observant) that can be applied to each individual in order to produce positive emotional and physical experiences that cause "feelings" of joy, peace, happiness, self-control, kindness, hopefulness, and love to be the "normal" expression of existence within a particular human condition? Is it universal in its application when applied with vigor and purposeful direction? Do we need to actually be cognitive about what we are doing, or can it happen by osmosis?

Sorry, it will take effort and purpose and focus to get the conductor of these machines we call bodies into line with the desires of the one who must gain control over this intellectual hot rod.

I was once told that if you took a beautifully manicured park with all its flowers and fountains and wooden walkways and left it unattended for one year, it would be overgrown with weeds and in disrepair. Anything left to itself without any attention to a desired conclusion will just naturally return to wilderness. This point is well made in South America, where they are finding whole cities encased in the jungle, whole civilizations overgrown with the wild components of a natural state that is left unattended. We need to attend to ourselves; we need to recognize what is correct and good and cultivate these qualities into our own beings (our intellectual souls and our hearts/spirits).

Professionals who say we are the way we are simply because we learned this behavior by close association with others make some pretty good points about how our behavior can be influenced by what we see and hear. That behavior proves successful in reaching a desired goal. The human condition demands attention if it is to succeed in an existence compatible with societal living. With moral rules comes conformity, with conformity comes peace, and with peace comes the possibility of vast populations living within close proximity to one another.

But how is this process taught from generation to generation? Is it simply taught by example, or is it acquired through purposeful cognitive intervention on the part of someone who has authority over a child? It is my opinion that if left to themselves individuals become overgrown with the "weeds" of an antisocial personality. If they are left to depend on their own thinking and the conclusion that this undirected thought breeds in individual thinking only resembles the conformity necessary to live within a community, merely surface compliance to the laws we all need to honor to coexist, then it is only a matter of time until they don't want to play the compliant role any longer. There actually are moral foundations that all children need to internalize within themselves so they might take a less destructive path in life, a path that will allow them to have productive and socialized lives filled with meaning and hope.

Psychology doesn't only try to keep count of what went wrong within an individual's life, but it tries to account for the thoughts that led to such a different way of thinking as to cause distress and dysfunction in the person's relationships to others around him or her. Psychologists then, when called upon by the individual, proceed to try to help him or her change his or her patterns of thinking in order to give him or her a healthy strategy for coexistence with others.

Where do psychologists get this strategy? Do they just make it up as they go along, or is there empirical research to support their claims about what an individual needs to change in order to live a relatively stress-free, anxiety-free existence? Is it true that the only thing we as humans need to fear is fear itself?

Misconceived ideas about what the future holds—misinterpretations about future events based on superficial evidence—sends our minds off into the land of confused thoughts and apprehensive emotions. What do we as human beings "think" the prerequisites for happiness and peace are? Who has set the standards in our minds and thoughts about what is necessary to be fulfilled? Are these standards so fleeting and arbitrary as to be prescribed by the ever-changing attitudes of society? Do we form our attitudes from ever-changing social platitudes?

The answer is that there is no foundation for a healthy life in the triteness of imposed social thinking through the repetition of meaningless babble thrown at the populace from numerous opinions that happen to be center-stage socially at any given time. The saying that if you don't believe in something, you'll fall for anything is pretty much on the mark. Moral foundations are needed to guide individuals in a steady direction with ever-increasing knowledge about the right and wrongs of human behavior. These moral foundations are not relative to time and space, but rather they are eternally established and significant at any time in a human life.

Foundational acceptance of moral foundations that are based in the absolute assurance that we can as people know what is "right" and what is "wrong" are categorical imperatives for an unconfused and less stressful lifestyle. It is not the fact that there are moral absolutes that brings distress into people's thoughts and lives; it is the rejection of what is inertly known as correct that brings distress to individuals. With this in mind, psychologists attempt through empirical findings to give individuals a leg up on appropriate thinking so that they don't need to take a lifetime to figure it all out by themselves.

Yet, it seems that society as a whole, and individuals in particular, want to reinvent the wheel all over again, along with all the bumps and ruts and dangerous intersections involved in the development stages. The shame of it is that while this generation is in the experimental stages of developing new moral absolutes, they have by their sides the next generation that is watching and listening and absorbing and taking as their own standards of behavior these flawed hypotheses as a proven theory. But it is not a proven anything, unless of course you use the absolute destructive behavior of a whole generation as outcome-based data for the failure of a perverted experiment in establishing new moral conduct free from any personal restraints. Seems the id has finally managed to get the ego and super ego neatly wedged into what must actually be a corner of the modern mind. How can you intervene in the thought patterns of a mind that laughs at the idea that anybody really needs to act in any kind of a uniform pattern of behavior in order to have a life worth living?

If a person is screaming in mental pain and absolutely out of control in his or her emotions, what do you tell him or her to help him or her get his or her life and emotions in order? Or do you simply drug him or her up and send him or her home to stare out his or her window? Can you intervene through language? Communication of concepts and ideas they people might weave into their unseen world of thoughts, the intangible forces individuals generate that cruise through the pathways of their minds, setting off chemical signals in unexplored areas of their minds that trigger the verbal and motor responses that are destroying them? We need not simply cut off the receptors that are receiving these signals, thus leaving the individual an emotionally dead battery, but rather we need to stop the erroneous flow of chemical interactions that steals his or her positive emotions and leaves him or her in a desert with a desperate thirst for a life he or she observes in others but are untrained to attain himself or herself—an abundant life.

Normal thought patterns—those thoughts that have a pattern of logically learned experiences in regard to "peace of mind" for an individual—are thoughts that are entertained by the individual without regard to the actions or behaviors that must proceed from thought that is accepted as *truthful and without error* in regard to how they relate to *beneficial actions and consequences* on the part of the "thinker." Thoughts generally precede actions; it is the thought that triggers purposeful biochemical actions within the brain once the concept is derived in the mind; the chemical responses to thought initiate purposeful movement. There is speculation about which comes first, whether (1) the brain through a predisposition generated from past experience simply automatically releases energy to specific areas of the body in reaction to sensory perceptions, or whether (2) the mind through conscious and unconscious determination of events actually directs the brain to proceed with its chemical output to achieve a predetermined course of events generated within the mind.

Can a person do intricate tasks without any awareness of the events preceding his or her decision to act in a prescribed manner? And if the possibility for such actions to take place exists, where is the power to express this action derived from? Is it derived from present thoughts? Or is it derived from stored information that exerts its influence when an experience opens the door for these thoughts to take actions that cause the implementation of biochemical reactions that are as inappropriate as the thought that generated them?

I have a drawer in my mental filing cabinet that is full of material that is erroneous in its conclusions and downright self-serving in its findings regarding many given topics. I have it filed specifically as nonfactual material—self-serving, erroneous hypotheses built on false findings bent to achieve an aim which the authors felt were "good" or felt any means justified the ends. If an individual were to find this file and not recognize that everything it presented was erroneous and then that individual proceeded to make decisions based on this information, he would soon find himself at the crossroads of several dead-end streets. On his way to this intersection, he would probably appear to others as ignorant rather than merely misinformed.

It is my opinion that each of us has a similar filing cabinet in the depths of our minds. And that file has a big sign on the front of it stating, *Stop! Make no decision based on this information.* If thoughts can generate energy that triggers biochemical events, then erroneous thoughts can generate energy that can cause erroneous actions, whether physical or simply adding more erroneous information to the concepts and beliefs generated from a concept that was false to begin with. If an individual collects and stores information within the confines of his mind and then holds these thoughts within the storage capacity of the brain, filed under "correct experiences," he leaves himself open to the fact that the brain may act on these "false truths" and generate a perverted logic in accordance with what it has trusted the mind to store for future logical thought. It is kind of similar to the idea that what we eat is what we are; garbage in equals garbage out. Erroneous storage of information equals erroneous logical perceptions accepted as truth.

In the late 1700s, a scientist by the name of Franz Anton Mesmer picked up a bit of knowledge from a Jesuit priest named Maximillian Hell (Mesmer, 1997). It seems that the power of suggestion had a strong influence on the physical symptoms of individuals when they were told what to expect from the psychological intervention they were about to receive for their physical ailments. (Hergenhahn, 1997, 449) Granted that many of these ailments are now considered to have been psychosomatic (of, relating to, or caused by the interaction of mental and bodily phenomena) in nature. The patients suffered from physical ailments caused by an error in the mind, an error of thought that manifested itself in the physical realm through the base information the brain used to create physical chemical responses to false information.

The mind does not clearly label areas of false experiences perceived as truth or unfounded ideas based in human fantasy that the mind has not determined to be true or false at the moment. Therefore the brain cannot tell the difference. When the mind has not as yet made a determination whether a block of information deserves to be classified as having validity, the brain presumes it to be true and generates energy and actions of both future storage of similar information and assumes the truthfulness of similar information generated within the imagination of the mind. This whole network develops in a way that reinforces itself by itself, and a stronghold is developed in the mind—a stronghold of false information considered by the brain to be factual and true. Once this stronghold gains a root in the brain, it becomes difficult for the mind to dislodge it from the brain's consideration in opposition to what the mind may then try to store as opposing information. The contradictions of mental thought and proper storage of corrected information in a network that is contradictory to this new information can cause a paradox for the brain. Square pegs can't go into round holes.

To start a new file for this now accepted alternative to the previously accepted hypothesis causes a contradiction within the brain. When searching for the proper emotional or physical responses to a given situation, which file does the brain use as its base of information to determine the proper biochemical sequences to activate to generate a proper response within the flesh?

So, when an individual knows what he or she wants to do in a situation but finds that he or she can't overcome the impulses to do the opposite or at least to deviate from his or her true desire is, it is at the very least, frustrating. There are associated areas of the brain that are not in direct contact with the mind. The autonomic nervous system can't be waiting around for conscious signals for every process to take place to keep the human body alive. This is the same in animals and humans. The machine that generates and holds life together so that the mind may exist is in a real sense separate from the activities of the intellect, yet the intellect can cause changes within the subconscious system of chemical behavior when it sends erroneous electrical energy into a network that automatically takes such chemical signals and acts upon them in a way in which it has no control. The brain makes no judgment on whether the chemical signals it receives are true or false. It doesn't act; it can only react.

I am fully aware that I have, for myself, accepted the hypothesis that thoughts generate actions. I have fully accepted this as the truth and continue from this point with no regard to an alternate understanding. We now have a grasp of the difference between purposeful action, both physical and the controlling of our thoughts (guarding our minds). There is a difference between the chemical actions that need to take place in our flesh for our existence, which is no different than for any living thing, and the chemical actions that take place due to the influence of our intellect, which is absolutely different from that of any other living thing. There are laws that govern our physical bodies and direct its metabolism and self-efficacy. They create cravings to make sure the body is nourished and release chemicals throughout its systems to keep it in balance and healthy, and they do so all without intellectual involvement. We don't eat because we are hungry. We are hungry because we haven't eaten, and our bodies are quick to remind us of that fact. If we are starving, it is because we have either chosen not to consume food or because there is no food to consume. Sometimes this can happen because we don't recognize the food around us. People have reportedly been found dead from starvation while being surrounded by an abundance of edible substances, but they were ignorant of this fact and died.

Individuals are emotionally and physically distressed, and they are dying because of their own thinking and beliefs when the answer is also right in front of them. They too are unaware the answer is there. It's not far away. No one needs to go any great distance to bring it to them. It has been before mankind for a very long time, but we are ignorant by choice, not by chance.

When individuals get themselves caught up in depression and become fearful of facing another day, we consider them to be emotionally confused, unable to assess the situation in "realistic" terms. Though the situation may be justifiably unpleasant, meditating on the problem only causes the individual to become incapacitated against finding a solution to the situation. Negative thoughts and words tend to reinforce the negative emotional responses to positive strategies for either correcting the situation or enduring the situation in an emotionally positive frame of mind. If we accept the hypothesis that thoughts can exert a measure of control over the biochemical reactions of our physical bodies, then it follows that words have the same power, for we as human beings think in words that represent images in our mind. A child without knowledge of language thinks in experiential pictures, but once we become aware of the correlation between the image and the word, we no longer need the picture to precede the thought. Words become the vehicle of the imagination and determine our physiological responses to a given idea or experience. Words have power. They plant seeds either of a sympathetic nervous response or a parasympathetic response.

In today's society, this hypothesis is considered archaic and foolish, at least among the so-called intellectuals of this generation. To them, the belief that words having any power over an individual borders on being a belief in demonology. However, thought and language are intimately connected, and together they rule the imagination, which in reality is the sum of our perception of any given circumstance. Experience may be the cause of us being the way we are.

But don't allow experiences to become an excuse to stay that way. Don't allow experiences to dictate attitudes. In *With Good Reason: An Introduction to Informal Fallacies,* a university-level text by S. Morris Engel, Mr. Engel states,

> *The relationship between language and thoughts is an age-old question. In the past, two views were dominant: one held that language is merely the vehicle or outer garment of thought; the*

> *other maintained that the stream of language and the stream of thought are one, that thought is merely soundless speech.*
>
> *More recently, research has tended to confirm the view that language and thought are intimately connected, that language is not merely sound but a union of sound and sense in which each is highly dependent on the other. Modern theories hold that words without thought are indistinguishable from other sounds to be found in nature. Such theories maintain, however, that, although we may have "vague thoughts" or ideas which we are unable to put into words, we cannot have a clear thought without being able to express it in language.* (Engel, 1994, 50)

Simply stated, thus, the wider the vocabulary the more expanded the ability to imagine ideas and concepts; the deeper the labyrinth of neurological pathways and associative networks that can trigger biochemical discharges creating physiological responses. Whether they be excitatory or inhibitory depends on the content of the thought expressed and held in the immediate consciousness.

Words are power. Whether they are used to destroy or build up is in the "will" of the thinker. But where is the meditation? Is there such a thing as the power of positive thinking? Are our thoughts self-fulfilling prophesies? Yes is the answer to both questions. As individuals, we "will" things to happen each and every day of our lives. Muscle responses are an act of our will when we simply think about moving across a room or picking up an object. Our thoughts cause the compliance of our physical bodies through electrochemical responses. We have the thought, and the action follows.

As unpopular as the word "religion" is in today's political climate, it should be mentioned that the concept of positive thinking is fundamentally a Christian truth, not simply epistemological but also experienced in the physical realm. Christianity has come under assault in the United States since the turn of the twentieth century, and we as a moral Christian people have gone straight downhill ever since.

Now, granted almost all true "religions" have many things in common. Few, if any, profess greed, murder, unbridled sexual gratification, lying, or cheating others as socially positive within a society. Where is this restraint on our thoughts and actions supposed to come from? Do individuals act a certain morally acceptable way solely out of fear of lawful punishment or do they act that way because they come to realize there is a way to "think" and "act" that is beneficial to them as autonomous individuals? It should be noted that Christianity, in its expression of moral and personal beliefs, is at its heart not a religion; it is a relationship with the Creator of all things through His Son Jesus Christ. This is not a philosophical concept. Religion by its nature is comparable to manmade laws, with its *dos* and *don'ts* for righteousness's sake. It is working one's way into a right relationship with God; however, the personage of God is understood within the many different "religions" of the world. Condemnation for deviation from these rules and laws is a common manipulation that is used to restrict behavior of individuals within a religious community.

Duty for duty's sake alone

Laws are only made for lawbreakers. To try to make this point clear, an individual would have to ask himself what he would do if he had the opportunity as an adult male to have a sexual relationship with several young girls in their early teens without any possibility of the physical contact ever becoming public knowledge. If his answer was yes, he would take advantage of these young girls, knowing he'd never be called to give account of his actions. Then the only restraint on his behavior would be the law and how he views the imposed restrictions. On the other hand, if his answer was no he would not take advantage of these young ladies because he knows within himself that they are vulnerable and not simply his for the taking to gratify his own lust, then he is not under the law. The law does not apply to him. He is not a lawbreaker in this regard.

Perceiving oneself as under a code or law to control what should be "normal" conduct can bring frustration to bear in the thought life of the individual. Studies have shown that the beliefs an individual holds within his personal inward schema wouldn't be easily changed by circumstance or peer pressure. Those behaviors that are simply repressed by "fear" of law or regulation will manifest themselves when the individual perceives he will not be held accountable for his actions by any higher authority. Then he will gleefully engage in such restricted behavior.

Christianity is a relationship with God that is not based in law but in an understanding of what is morally right and good and an understanding of what is morally wrong and destructive. When this cognitive network is clearly defined within an individual's mind and held without confusion as to whether there are such things as absolutes regarding civilized thinking and behavior, he has no frustration at not being able to satisfy his every lust. This is because the decision to not engage in morally wrong behavior is restrained by the light of the truth, not because of the law but rather because of an understanding of what is right and good for the intellect and the soul to have a peaceful existence within his body.

The body will respond to right thinking once the "positive" networks are established within the individual. We as individuals can do what our minds know will produce a productive and rewarding lifestyle, or we can answer the debased nature of physical impulses and through the consequences of unrestrained behavior simply destroy ourselves in a quagmire of confused, so-called enlightenment. The decision is the individual's, and there are many different philosophies fighting for control of the minds of the youth of this country. For indeed, the hand that rocks the cradle controls the world in the next generation, not through brainwashing but through brain pollution that becomes the inert thinking of the next generation.

So we don't need to give up one type of slavery—adherence to manmade laws that change on a whim—for the slavery of religion that binds the minds of individuals as tightly as any secular legal system. To have a healthy thought life that will manifest itself into a successful life of relationships and kindness toward others, one need only to not lean on his or her own thinking but trust what the greatest psychologist ever known had to say in what is simply referred to as "Holy" scriptures.

This concept doesn't sit well with social humanists, who really do detest any possibility that someone might actually adhere to such a principle as the "truth" of God's Word. If you're having an epistemological problem with the word *God*, then simply try to get your intellect to substitute the concept of an *ultimate loving authority* in your neurological network, with an understanding that this authority only has your best interests at heart. This authority is not the "power" of a *Star Wars*, the-force-be-with-you mentality, but rather an individual who is alive within another realm and reaching out to His creations to help guide them to a human existence full of peace, joy, love, happiness, kindness, and faithfulness. His guidance is based not in laws but rather in personal knowledge and wisdom free from debased erroneous paradigms. It is based in a personal understanding of what is right and what is wrong, free from the interference of physical animal desires and more in line with the desired human nature—a healthy biochemical direction of thought patterns governed by "love" and not by self-gratifying lust.

A scientific paradigm fostered in a fallacious belief in the evolution of the human race from the animal kingdom has corrupted our present-day intellect. Assumptions built on a false hypothesis that has been accepted as scientific fact out of a desire for unrestrained personal biases can only lead to other erroneous conclusions. These conclusions, based on erroneous foundations, are like a house of cards; when the foundation finally goes, the whole lie will crumble.

A foundation built on self-actualization and the unrestrained desire for self-determination will foster selfish, unrestrained behavior among deceived individuals. It fosters destructive, self-serving behavior disguised as personal freedom. Immanuel Kant put it rather well in his writing on the *Critique of Practical Reason* when he stated that "… morality is not properly the doctrine of how we should make ourselves happy, but how we should become worthy of happiness" (Kant, 1995, 74).

Is "correct" (having a positive affect both socially and individually) behavior learned by modeling, or is it cognitive (taught)? I would put forth the proposition that in today's America, it is neither exhibited nor taught within an educational setting out of fear of obedience to some ancient supposed superstition, namely Christianity as an inspired truthful guide to abundant life both individually and socially. Now, I realize I'm entering an area that for some reason stirs up emotional turmoil for many pseudointellectuals. It seems no one likes or will tolerate any restrictions on personal behavior.

The era of all individuals coming to a truth of their own has really produced a mentally unhealthy mass of individuals in America. By almost all accounts, we are a psychological mess when it comes to the mental health of the people as a group. In fact, if we take all the statistics generated by professionals engaged in treating different mental disorders among the population, there only seems to be two individuals who are unaffected: me and you. It has been said that religious principle is the culprit when it comes to "putting guilt" on individuals, which causes them to be distressed mentally. There are those who feel that an understanding or right and wrong is somehow the cause for mental distress among those who would participate in a lifestyle someone else might call deviant. They say no one has the right to force others to live up to a moral code that is not one they believe in. In other words, there are no moral absolutes, and there should be no "laws" against any behavior within a society that doesn't hurt anyone and is of mutual consent between supposedly enlightened adults.

People really get an attitude when it comes to "moral" absolutes that uplift a society but aren't within the intellectual capacity for some individuals to understand beyond their own petty lust and desires. The way we "think" is the direct barometer of how we "behave," and the way we "act" is who we become. Act the way you want to be. The only problem is that so many individuals want to be a way that is contrary to a civilized (refined, polished) society. No one seems to have a compass for direction, and no one wants to be handed one that might require any restraint on personal desires that have ingrained themselves in the "thoughts" and "words" that have created a lifestyle of destruction. The *Star Trek* and *Star Wars* pseudospirituality is nothing more than cosmic Eastern religion, merely human philosophy lost in the aberrant fantasies of human intellect. People want the right to destroy themselves and demand the right to take others with them by perverting others' thinking with vain philosophies and utter nonsense based on false assumptions, sheer fantasies based in the thinking of a naturalistic material world.

Now you might ask yourself, "What was that last paragraph all about in relationship to mental distress?" Well, before I try to make clear to someone the relevancy of Christian understanding of the situation of mental distress, I feel compelled to address an area that seems to be a favorite for intellectual justification for debunking religious (Christian) statements, specifically in the realm of demons and the devil.

Can delusions affect an individual's behavior? Do delusions have substance in regard to affecting behavior? A delusion manifests itself in altered personal behavior as much as any medication may affect a change in individual behavior. Medical changes may be deemed positive if they eliminate the delusional responses to the environment, yet the thoughts that lead to erroneous thinking (delusions) are generally considered negative. Associated thoughts that cruise neurological networks and affect perceptions of physical reality are as substantive as any reality based in physical experience. Erroneous thoughts can kill, steal, or destroy the quality of an individual's life, and by doing so they become an invisible reality that can be measured in terms of an observable destructive outcome. As with the antisocial personality disorder (APD), the measurement of condition is derived from the destruction around the individual's life; it is not necessarily measured against what the individual sees as destructive but rather the consequences of the individual's behavior. You can call the condition disruptive neurological activity, or you can call these erroneous thoughts "demons." Choose whichever term your intellectual capacity is capable of handling; both descriptive terms convey the same mental condition.

I assume that if you're still with me, you have an understanding of religious concepts and their relevance in some regard to civilized cultures. Now, I realize our intellectual community in America is dysfunctional regarding what must be taught to the upcoming generations if we are to survive as a nation. But common sense is forever being called religious in nature. If it wasn't so sad, the fact would be almost funny. We can't have the Ten Commandments on the walls of our schools because someone might read them and then somehow be motivated to believe a religious concept. Meanwhile, of course, children are gunning down their classmates at lunchtime and recess. I won't get into the fact that the thoughts and words these children saturate their minds with each and every day by cognitively entertaining their surroundings under the guise of "freedom of expression" goes directly to their expression of the language and thoughts that permeate their little minds. I don't care if you can prove it empirically or not; if empirical facts are necessary and common sense is discarded when "facts" can't be presented in a so-called appropriate "scientific format," we as a people really become a bunch of buffoons.

Anyway, back to the point. Throughout literature there are writings that are read and understood at different levels of sophistication. Earlier, I put forth a statement that you can't comprehend beyond your ability within a given language. An understanding of words used in a piece of writing is necessary to obtain deeper than a surface understanding of statements made with regard to "sound and sense." So to simply disregard the "thought" of demons as a "force" within the mental concepts of an individual who is experiencing aberrant feelings and exhibiting deviant behavior is to miss an understanding that, for the pseudointellectual, may seem mythical in nature. But to someone with an understanding of how thought can generate biochemical reactions that can lead to electrical energy released within the synapse of the brain, the release of an unseen force that causes an individual to exhibit behavior that he or she may very well not want to exhibit but consciously cannot control may seem like a the-devil-made-me-do-it occurrence.

How many obsessive-compulsives might make such a statement? Or for that matter, how many diagnosed schizophrenics might make the same statement? So when you read about demons, don't limit your understanding to that of a pseudointellectual, but rather try to understand the concept through so-called scientific advancements that have been made through intellectual inquiry over the past century. Try not to be so intellectually bigoted as to be intellectually blind to the concepts expressed to the world over twenty centuries ago by someone who knew exactly what forces were at work in this world but had an audience that neither had the language nor the understanding to make such a connection.

Twenty centuries ago, that audience was unable to understand beyond the fact that unseen forces can influence individuals and cause physical problems. They could only obtain a level of understanding of the concepts that was equivalent to what could be expressed through their present-day language. At that time and place, with that language and sense, the concept of demons was sufficient to express what the presence of the unseen world of neurological activity and the influence an aberrant chemical balance could cause in an individual's thinking.

So when you read a Christian concept such as the "devil" only comes to steal, kill, and destroy, try to remember that these three things are in fact the prevalent outcomes of mental illness. Mental illnesses indeed kill, steal, and destroy. So let us try to get past our higher educational brainwashing regarding "religious" concepts; foolishness lies in the ignorance of expressing knowledge in a format that an intellectual person would understand only after pursuing the facts of a statement by examining it in light of the language and zeitgeist of the time period, brought together in the present for a deeper understanding than could be realized by a two-thousand-year-old audience with limited ability to intellectually comprehend the concept.

So let us leave the demonology behind us and go on to the power of positive Christian thinking in the life of an individual who is confused and distressed within the concepts of the twentieth-century life experience. The truth remains the truth, regardless of time and space. It is not dependent on whether it is culturally liked or individually grasped; truth is always true.

A leading authority once asked the question, "What is truth?" The authority was answered by a man who would later rise from the grave, rise from the dead. "I am the truth," was the man's answer. "No one gets to God except through me"(John 14:6 NIV).

An individual's spiritual essence (self as knower) must be changed, must be connected to the universal Creator, the One who created all things by design and with purpose (not *Star Wars* or *Star Trek* theology). As popular as it is for our own desires to be in charge of our actions and the thinking that precedes these actions, the human race is ill-suited to understand any foundational absolutes as a basis for the formulation of ideas and concepts that might lead to an understanding of foundational principles. These principles are needed for an obedient (attention to the details that make an individual worthy to receive happiness) existence within the reality of this physical universe. Where we place our intellectual acceptance will determine the networks of thought that we not only generate but also propagate.

Chapter 5

Resurrection through Reconciliation: Putting Death to Death—Motive, Means, and Opportunity

Motive, means, and opportunity—these three factors are generally given as the necessary conditions for surmising that an individual could be a suspect in the premeditated death of another individual. I would propose to you that these same factors are necessary for the resurrection of the dead. Affording someone the opportunity to go from death to life is by no means a task that can be taken for granted. As is the case with a physical death, those who are dead really do not know they are dead. Individuals who have come to know the truth of the reality of the human condition in its relationship with the Creator through receiving the gift of His Spirit through faith in His Son are mandated to share this Good News with those who are dead and to encourage fellow believers who have received this New Life.

Someone might wonder why one human being should be concerned about another human being's present and eternal life? What is the motive? The motive is love fired by compassion.

There is a risk for those who seek true love. You see, love doesn't look to receive; it longs to be poured out. When true love comes to find a place in the very heart and spirit of the individual, the journey that one takes can sometimes be a lonely journey. Mankind not only desires to love but also to be loved in return.

Unselfish love is not the natural order of things in this existence. Unselfish love is a gift from God, poured out into those who have come to know God on a very personal level through vibrant faith in what His Son accomplished for us at Calvary. It is not head knowledge; it is heartfelt. The love of God has been poured out into our hearts by the Holy Spirit. God loves us even when we are unlovable.

Our motives to raise the dead are exactly the same as our Father's motive to raise us from the dead—so that we might have fellowship with Him and be one with our brothers and sisters in Christ through the same Holy Spirit that dwells in every believer. Each time a human is raised up from the deadness of a life separated from God, flesh is added to the Body of Christ in this natural world, and a spirit has come home for eternity through faith in Christ. There are many humans who are lost and separated from God in the depths of their souls; they perish even while they smile and laugh. Many are not laughing but languishing in a dark pit of existence, silently screaming out for someone to help them find peace in his souls. When Christ lives in you, the Power of the Holy Spirit, fired by the knowledge of the Word, brings a love within your heart that breeds the compassion of God for those who are lost. The compassion of Christ knows no bounds. It cries for the unlovable, it extends its hand to the unrighteous, and it extends a message that will heal all that ails mankind, both in body and in mind.

When the love of God shines through His Child, then His children's motives are to show each and every person that God has made a way home because He loves us and has compassion for us. That should be every believer's motive. Do we as believers have the means to actually raise the dead? Resurrection through reconciliation! There can be no resurrection without a death, and there can be no reconciliation until the debt is paid in full. What are the means by which this can possibly be accomplished?

Considering that the debt to be paid is eternal death, both physical and spiritual—for indeed no man is in right standing with God in his own right—what are the means to effect a resurrection from this death? The Good News! God has made a way!

Yes, we have the means to accomplish this resurrection by telling everyone what Jesus the Christ has told us to tell everyone throughout the whole world. You see, it is Jesus's message that has the power to change men's souls. It is the message, not the messenger, not the disciples! As believers we cannot save anybody, but we can tell them about the One who has made the way for them to come home to the Father.

> *For I am not ashamed of the Gospel (good news) of Christ, for it is God's power working unto salvation [for deliverance from eternal death] to everyone who believes with a personal trust and a confident surrender and firm reliance, to the Jew first and also to the Greek. For in the Gospel a righteousness which God ascribes is revealed, both springing from faith and leading to faith [disclosed through the way of faith that arouses to more faith]. As it is written, the man who through faith is just and upright shall live and shall live by faith.* (Rom. 1:16–17 AMP)

If indeed as believers we know that we have the tools and the directive to share the truth with others, then how should we proceed to deliver this mandate within our own spheres of influence? How do we recognize the specific opportunities that sometimes pass us by during our day-to-day, moment-by-moment sojourn through this reality of physical life? Webster defines opportunity as the favorable combination of circumstances, time, and place in regard to a chance for advancement or progress (*The New Merriam-Webster Dictionary* 1989, G.K. Hall & Co.). Recognizing an opportunity would be a reasonable first step in understanding how to take advantage of an opportunity.

Sometimes as corporate bodies, we endeavor to create opportunities for sharing our faith, and this is well and good. Getting together and formulating a plan of action for handing out tracks and seeking out those who have no real understanding of the Gospel is wonderful stuff, but it is limited in its scope. Should we as believers constantly be trying to create opportunities, or should we be more sensitive to the plights of others in our lives so that we become skilled through the power of the Holy Spirit to recognize and seize opportunities in the moment? In my opinion, both are necessary, but the latter offers more day-to-day opportunities. First, do the lives that we are living show forth anything that would make an unbeliever desire our input into their lives as a sound strategy for a more fulfilling existence?

Jesus says, "Behold, I stand at the door and knock; if anyone hears and listens to and heeds My voice and opens the door, I will come in to him and will eat with him, and he [will eat] with Me" (Rev. 3:20 AMP). So the question seems to be, whose voice are people hearing when we as believers share the Gospel of our Lord? Are they hearing our Lord's voice or just some religious rhetoric of judgment and condemnation?

John 3:16 (see appendix B) is a wonderful scripture that usually is one of the first scriptures a new believer sets down to memory, but let's not forget the crux of the matter mentioned in the next verse: "For God did not send His Son into the world to condemn the world, but that the world through Him might be saved" (John 3:17 NKJV).

In order to take advantage of any opportunity, it is important not only to recognize the opportunity but also to have the wisdom to be able to voice a solution. Whose voice is someone hearing when you speak to the ailments in their souls, the ailments that are stealing their very lives away? Is it the voice of condemnation from the enemy, or is it the voice of reconciliation from the Lord? Depending on who lives in you and has control of you will be the determining factor in whether your life reflects the freedom our Lord provides through His blood or whether it reflects the bondage of religion that our enemy provides through his deceptive counterfeit: religious exercises.

If you have a keen ear with which to hear, you will find opportunities to let your light shine in almost every interaction with others during the course of your daily routine. Don't let the judgmental attitude of religion cast a cloud over your spiritual mind and your inner voice of compassion and love for the lost. Don't be surprised by the behavior of those who are lost, and always remember the simple fact that they are *lost* and not only don't know the way home, but they aren't even looking for a way home. They think the misery they often find themselves engulfed in is a normal state of affairs. When you cast the light of the Gospel into their lives by the contrast of your life to theirs, they can see the difference. There needs to be a difference.

When the sharing of the Gospel of Jesus Christ becomes equated with a hate crime, I would hope there would be enough evidence against any sincere believer to find him or her extremely guilty as charged.

The way of the transgressor is hard, make no mistake about it. This is a true statement of fact from God's Word. To transgress is to go beyond the divine law of God, to exceed the boundaries set by God in our everyday activities, to sin (miss the mark).

Make no mistake about it, we all transgress, but without an understanding of the Gospel of Jesus the Christ, we have no recourse but to carry this weight. It is a heavy load to carry in our hearts and minds (souls). As believers, we have a way to receive forgiveness when we recognize our mistakes. We can recognize our mistakes in the light of God's Word and receive forgiveness when we fess-up, sincerely renew our minds to God's Word, and move away from the thoughts and behaviors that caused us to stumble into self-gratification and the unholy trinity of me, myself, and I. Individuals who have no recourse but to carry this weight of transgression begin to show it in their countenance. A keen ear and a keen eye will enable the Holy Spirit to trigger the very compassion of Christ in you to bring the medicine that heals the heart and mind of the transgressor: forgiveness.

You see, Jesus said He stands at the door of everyone's heart: "Behold, I stand at the door and knock; if anyone hears and listens to and heeds My voice and opens the door, I will come in to him and will eat with him, and he [will eat] with Me" (Rev. 3:20 AMP). As believers, we have the key that can prompt an unbeliever to open the door and let the Lord come into his or her heart and live His life through him or her. It is the Gospel that has the power to save everyone who believes.

It is not difficult to hear the torment in the voices of those who are walking in this world under their own power. You can see it through their plastic smiles and hear it through their hesitant expressions of vain hope for the future. They talk about a whole bunch of activities designed to get ahead in life, lots of action, lots of words, lots of dreams, all signifying nothing—no eternal purpose, just temporary gladness until this next defeat.

Remember that an opportunity is based on a favorable combination of circumstance, time, and place. No one comes to the Lord Jesus unless he or she is drawn to Him by the Holy Spirit. How does an unbeliever hear and learn of the Holy Spirit? Well, through exposure to Jesus through the lives of those in whom He lives today. Through the witness of those who have been set free from the law that causes those who transgress to carry their own load of mistakes and regrets. Faith comes by hearing the Word of God. Intimacy comes from spending time with God. The lifestyle and countenance of a believer should be in such contrast to those who walk in the natural as to be as glaring as a spotlight shining at the midnight hour. Words are cheap!

As parents raise children, the children learn quickly. Children may not always do what you say, but they will be sure to do as they see you do. Modeled behavior is a strong teacher and a witness to the inner most issues of the heart. This is not a small issue in regard to taking advantage of the right circumstance, place, and time to share your faith. When unbelievers are exposed to a professing follower of Jesus Christ, they should see a different type of person than they are used to seeing in their lives. Does this mean they should see some strict religious person who has a list of all the *dos* and *don'ts* that need to be followed in some work-orientated plan for acceptance before Father God? Emphatically not! If this is all they see, then when the circumstances of the brokenness of life without Jesus come upon them, they will run from you and right into the arms of secular humanism.

On the other hand, if what they have seen in your life is compassion instead of condemnation, kindness instead of judgment, love instead of anger, or a simple smile instead of a frown, the chance to share your faith at the right time in the right place when the storms of life descend upon them will indeed present itself. The Holy Spirit will draw them to the Christ in you that has transformed your life and shines through you to a troubled world. It has been said that when an individual dies, a whole universe dies with them. All their perceptions, all their day-to-day experiences within this reality, all their gazing upon this creation, all their wants and dreams and hopes die with them. A whole universe based from within them is extinguished, and then they get to move on to an eternity either of loneliness and torment within their very alive souls or one of happiness and joy where there are no tears in the presence of the Father of all creation through the blood of His Son who offers the only access to eternal life in His presence.

Where the Spirit of the Lord is, there is liberty. What exactly is liberty? Liberty is an action going beyond what is familiar. What is very familiar to all of us as human beings? Being carnal-minded is very familiar to the entire human race. In fact, it is something that as believers we must constantly be aware of in our lives. To be carnal-minded is to be mindful of the desires of the flesh and of its demands to be gratified. So to experience liberty in the carnal area is to be able to go beyond what is familiar in this arena by the power of the

Holy Spirit with joyfulness. So how do we react to circumstances in our lives? Carnally or spiritually? The desires of the carnal nature are listed in Galatians chapter 5, and the list is not exhaustive; it is simply directive.

Now, I don't want to get too far a field from the point of your life drawing individuals toward the Christ in you. However, if we lack an understanding of how the Holy Spirit can make our lives shine way beyond what is familiar to unbelievers, why would they seek out the liberty and freedom we claim to possess through the Spirit and Word of God if we act and react in a manner that is all too familiar to them?

Take, for instance, anger (the flesh, generally). Do you have to bite your tongue in order to not respond in an angry way, or has the Word of God so impregnated your heart that anger doesn't ever get the chance to raise its ugly little head? Don't ever think that your countenance doesn't reveal your heart, even when you don't say any words. When your whole being is bathed in the liberty Christ offers, His light shines through your countenance with the brilliance of the Son.

How about sexual lust? It is very carnal and very familiar (common) in all generations. What do unbelievers see in a believer that is unfamiliar to them in this area? Manipulation of another person's emotions through purposeful enticement and exploitation of the innate desires of the flesh is a brief definition of the elements of witchcraft. Speaking as a male (though this applies to females also), I would say that liberty in this area is hard fought: meat not milk. For men, to be able to interact with the opposite sex in liberty is to look on younger women as their sisters and older women as their mothers. They do so from a regenerated heart and mind that stops the carnal instinct of their physiology to transfer the blood from their brains to the only single member of the five appendages of the male anatomy (ladies have a less obvious transfer). When a man has mastered this difficult proposition, he has indeed begun to experience liberty (the unfamiliar) in this area. Thank the Holy Spirit in you, for He gives the power to change.

The liberty Jesus offers in all areas will get the attention of the unbeliever. When the circumstances are right in unbelievers' lives, they will find the place and make the time to seek out the liberty they see in you. Then you will have the opportunity to share what and who has set you free from the bondage of everyday life in this reality. You will share in words and with the power to change someone's life. Who can offer a message of hope and liberty through the freedom of grace by faith if he or she is bound by religion in his or her own life? Don't be like the foolish Galatians and turn from the truth. You are saved by grace through faith.

So are you guilty of being a Christian? The Word of God has given you the means, the love of God has given you the motive, and a dying world will offer the opportunity when you are sensitive to the prompting of the Holy Spirit. When you hold Him up in your life, He will draw others to you. Stand strong in the faith in the face of opposition. Jesus tells us not to take it personally:

> *If the world hates you, you know that it hated Me before it hated you. If you were of the world, the world would love its own. Yet because you are not of the world, but I chose you out of the world, therefore the world hates you. Remember the word that I said to you, "A servant is not greater than his master." If they persecuted Me, they will also persecute you.* (John 15:18–20 NKJV)

Section II

But I say, walk and live [habitually] in the [Holy] Spirit [responsive to and controlled and guided by the Spirit]; then you will certainly not gratify the cravings and desires of the flesh (of human nature without God). For the desires of the flesh are opposed to the [Holy] Spirit, and the [desires of the] Spirit are opposed to the flesh (godless human nature); for these are antagonistic to each other [continually withstanding and in conflict with each other], so that you are not free but are prevented from doing what you desire to do.

—Galatians 5:16–17, AMP

Chapter 6

Cultural Engineering: Up from the Ashes

If you jump on the horse or sit on the seat, you will pay the price of admission. And the spinning never stops.

It's a wild ride—when your life is in a tailspin. We will never be able to regain a focus on our previous dreams and heartfelt desires. All is lost in a reality spinning out of control just beyond our field of vision, going by so fast that we barely recognize all those things that were once so familiar and meaningful. Now they are lost in a blurring of faces and fragmented consciousness. People laugh, and the music plays on, but reality stands still and there is no longer any comfort beyond the ride. That one step into the false joys and momentary happiness of this folly has now separated us from our very lives, and we don't know how to get home again. Plastic smiles and futile hopes mark our very existence, yet we keep returning to the wheel of momentary pleasure even while we decay and rot from the inside out—physically, mentally, and spiritually.

If you have "bought a ticket to ride," I assure you that you will not like the eventual destination; it is full of misery beyond description and can only be appreciated in all its horror through experience.

What is this ride, you might ask. I don't ride on merry–go-rounds! You may not even know you've bought that ticket to ride. You may be so busy keeping your focus on your hopes and dreams that you haven't noticed the rest of reality flashing past, just out of reach.

In a counseling psychology class, I once heard a professor make the statement that we were going to learn how to be altruistic and empathetic. In reality, that is a pretty funny statement. I asked him if he wasn't sure he really meant to say we were going to learn how to *act* in these particular manners. To be altruistic is to have an unselfish interest in the welfare of others, and to be empathetic is to have the capacity of experiencing as one's own the feelings of another. An individual who has these attributes is an individual who understands the emotional impact circumstances/situations have on another individual.

I would put to you that these qualities are learned from a very young age through modeling and experiencing the rewards of such attributes in an individual's inner being. To say that these core beliefs can be taught at a later time in life is a fallacy. Can they become part of a person's inner being later in life? No, they cannot by definition, not when the acquisition of these qualities is motivated by self-interest. So to say I want to learn how to *act* this way in order to help others is not the same as saying I want to *be* this way because it is the right way to be.

Up from the ashes

If you observed someone who had accidentally lit themselves on fire, would you not try to extinguish the flames? Are we not taught as little children that fire and extreme heat can be destructive? Is there not knowledge that is so important that it must be passed on to our young children to protect them from harm?

Ashes are the residue left behind by something that has been destroyed by fire or extreme heat. Generally, ashes are of no use to anyone. They are discarded. If by chance the heat has not been applied for a long enough time, the destruction of the burned object may not be complete. In the midst of the ashes, there might still remain the essence of the object.

Anyone familiar with burning wood for heat will attest to this fact. There can be a raging fire at some point, but sometimes in the morning when you go to stoke the fire, you will find that some wood has indeed not been consumed. Have you ever burned stacks of newspaper in a fire? If the stacks were left undisturbed while burning, you found paper and print deep in the middle of the stacks that had not been burned.

In the midst of the ashes, something still remained to attest to the original character of the item burned. Out of the ashes, something still remained and was retrievable.

Out of the ashes of the present-day American culture, I would put to you that there remains something retrievable. This something has almost been destroyed by the destructive heat of secular humanism, secular as in "the absence of the reality of God." Secular thinking is a merry-go-round of folly, never-ending self-interest disguised as self-actualization, glorification of the part at the expense of the whole, a hatred of the idea of accountability to anyone other than the self. Secular thinking is an end-justifies-the-means ideology.

Destruction is as culture teaches

It has been a long time in coming—the destruction we see rampant throughout the American culture today. Is it really true that there is no right or wrong? Are these concepts of right and wrong merely subjective to an individual at the time and relative to the situation and the law of a given society of that time? If such is the case, then who is accountable for individual behavior—the individual or the society?

If there were no laws, there would be no lawbreakers. So is it the law that makes people seem out of the "social norms" of behavior relative to their own actions? Is it the fault of the law? At this point in time, it seems that the focus of the "social elitists" is not so much to make new laws but rather to overturn existing laws. They say it is necessary because society is always changing and that laws must reflect the feelings and beliefs of the people it governs.

What is going on here? Have the inmates actually taken over the asylum? It is beginning to appear as if that is indeed the case. In America, laws are supposed to be made through Congress. Yet it seems laws are now being made by lunatic judges who have somehow gained positions of judicial power. Even our Supreme Court has been infiltrated by so-called progressive thinkers.

We as a people should not really be surprised. The seeds for all this confusion were planted a long time ago in the educational system of America. There are still some strong fibers in the "ashes" of that system, but you would have to dig to find them. The intellectuals who are in charge of educating our children have themselves been diverted over time in their own educational endeavors; they have become the robots of destructive social ideologies founded in the lunacy of the triad of me, myself, and I theology.

It now seems that anything that is perceived as a moral absolute is somehow religious in nature and to be ignored or, more preciously, shunned. Actually, that really is a great vote of confidence for religious people. I mean, when the society is going down in flames and the society is adamant about not hearing anything perceived as religious in its foundational understanding of right and wrong, the destructive end verifies the lack of knowledge of the means to change it from its self-inflicted demise.

For example, "religious" people would say that temperance is necessary when using alcohol because alcohol leads to uncontrolled thinking and behavior. Now society simply says, "Don't drive." The destruction caused by the misuse of alcohol is obvious to any thinking person. "Religious" individuals would say physical intimacy belongs between a man and a woman to build a foundation for the rearing of physically and socially healthy offspring. Society says, "Don't get pregnant (until you've completed your career goals), don't catch diseases (you will transmit them to all your other contacts), and if you do get pregnant by mistake, get an abortion." We wouldn't want any fatherless children running around unattended. There were at one time laws against this socially destructive behavior. Not anymore.

Some people say there are too many people in prisons on drug offenses. They say, "Let's make recreational drugs legal and the crime rate will drop." Duh. Doesn't take a genius to figure that one out. By the same token, there are too many sex offenders in prison. Why not just have some judge lower the age of consent between "sexually mature" individuals? Then as a society, we can apologize collectively to all the misunderstood child molesters who have been incarcerated.

After all, if a twelve-year-old girl can make the decision to have an abortion without telling her parents or guardian, then why can't she decide who to have sex with in the first place? If same-sex unions/ contracts are now given credibility as healthy relationships, who is to tell a sexually mature post-adolescent young man (thirteen years old) that he can't have a homosexual relationship with a much older, mature man (thirty-five years old)? Who has the right to dictate anything to anybody, even at the cost of a society built on Christian moral principles?

I guess if a law inhibits someone's behavior on moral grounds, then that idea is somehow religious and therefore discarded. I personally think that everything that is good and wholesome is considered religious because that is the only way secular humanists can cancel it out and make it of no regard within the social system they are trying to implement. Religion interferes with sexual fantasies. Talk about hedonism.

Stop the fire: no such thing as sexual morality

If homosexuals are born that way, what about pedophiles? Does society have a right to protect itself from destructive aberrations? What or who determines the age of consent? Paganism is reasserting itself into society. Everything is up for grabs. It is godless behavior.

Don't be deceived. It is a homosexual agenda, and it's in media, in education, in corporate structures, in entertainment—both TV and cinema. It is all about perversion as the norm. Once it is the norm, it no longer can qualify as a perversion.

But what is normal? It is what the majority considers acceptable based on nothing more than personal preference. In India, it is still relatively normal for newborn baby girls to either disappear or simply die at birth. It is normal in America for a person to deal with the consequences of sexual activity by killing a baby before it can be born. Taking a drug that stops a fertilized egg from implanting in the uterus wall is killing a potential human being. Actually, it is not a potential human being; it is a human being with potential. It is interfering with the "normal" development of this person as he or she moves through the "normal" cycle of development.

It is the same on the other end of the cycle. To put someone to death because it has been decided that he or she cannot live a "normal" quality of life is just as depraved. But of course, once older people become "useless eaters," they also become a drain on the resources of a society and steal from the next generation, which has a right to eliminate them for the national good. Sound familiar anyone? It's just another attempt at culture cleansing—old idea, new tyrants.

Chapter 7

The Sexing up of Our Children: Back to Rome BC

As a society we really have become something of a pathetic group of self-centered individuals. We've isolated ourselves in a stockyard of ignorant and valueless opinions to the demise of the lives of those who will follow us into the future.

There was a time when if you were inclined to entertain your perverse physical fantasies or mentally deprived imaginations of taboo pleasures, you needed to go into the darkest corners of our society to watch drug-addicted individuals demean themselves by engaging in live sexual acts on smelly old mattresses in some dingy room equipped with broken-down chairs and tissue paper rolls scattered about the viewing area. Now it seems that this behavior is simply part of our natural search for sexual fulfillment, and it can be found on the school buses that transport our children to their learning institutions. And it doesn't include just those who participate in the sexual acts but also the roaring, applauding, approving crowd of adolescents who view such behavior as "normal."

Oh yeah, we really do need this generation of educators teaching young people how to get in touch with their sexuality. It seems that they are going to do it anyway. We can't have them all spayed, so let's just teach them to slap on a condom and go to it. How about oral sex? Oral sex isn't sex, or did you forget? Oral sex has just become the alternative to taking the risk of having to endure an abortion. Abortions are available to those who, in the heat of the moment, let their guard down and allowed someone to actually slip an unprotected genital in under their tail. When are we going to stop thinking of our offspring as nothing more than hormone-crazed animals? With dogs, any dog will do, and then the bitch stands alone.

What are the defining criteria for sexually "inappropriate behavior" these days? It seems as if it is only defined by the age of the participants. But this is an arbitrary criterion, is it not? On what basis is this criterion set? It was once based on an understanding of the term *morality*. Now it seems that there is no such concept as fundamental morality. As our "clone" friends tell us, morality is an individual, personal concept; it is different for everyone and clothed in in-group thinking, arbitrary at best and purposefully decadent at worst.

If the only thing defining appropriate sexual contact between consenting individuals is age difference and that age difference is set on some arbitrary moral concept, it is subject to change. Who will be in a position to make these changes? More then likely some of the individuals who were cheering on the individuals having oral sex on the school bus. If a twelve-year-old in the state of Florida can divorce his parents because he doesn't like the rules they impose on him and another a twelve-year-old can obtain an abortion without parental notification or approval, then why can't a twelve-year-old make the decision to have sexual contact with anyone he or she chose?

For society to say they can't, based on an arbitrary sense of morality, is inconsistent with the progressive thinkers who are sitting in positions of authority to make such legal rulings. As it stands now, adolescents can have sexual contact with others as long as there is no more than a four-year age difference, up to the age of eighteen. So the seventeen-year-old boy having sexual contact with his thirteen-year-old girlfriend is legal. When he turns eighteen and she turns fourteen, he becomes a sex offender. Do not be surprised when you hear that the age for sexual consent between an individual over eighteen has been lowered to the age of thirteen for the partner. I guess society will have a whole bunch of apologizing to do to all those uncles who got caught playing doctor with their (then) underage nieces.

I find myself constantly astounded by the fundamental idea that good behavior is somehow a religious concept. I don't think any father wants his daughter having sexual contact with his brother, even if that father is a confessed secular humanist. It seems we as a society are heading down the Roman road, back to the first century BC, which by the way now has been changed in many of our higher institutions to B.C.E. which means "before the common era." We no longer want Christ dividing historical time. You have to love those secular liberals. Even when the first century after the common era began it was a time in the then capital of the world, Rome, of no-holds-barred immorality. Anything went when it came to a sexual theme park of unrestrained mental and physical depravity. I mean, after all, if there is no such thing as morality, then what is the big deal? Dogs do it. Male dogs take no responsibility for their offspring. The pack pitches in, mostly the bitches. Sadly, they are stuck doing it because they were born with the nipples, I guess. It kind of mirrors the state of affairs we have developed through our mental apathy.

Hey, if you don't stand for something, you will fall for anything. I would suggest that those who have any sense of morality written on their hearts teach their grandchildren a sense of moral decency. The youth of today are not going to get any sense of Christian morality from what they hear out there in the world (i.e., media, movies, video games, school systems, colleges, universities, Internet, etc.). It seems the inmates having taken over the asylum are having an open house and almost everybody is coming and sitting at the feet of these pseudointellectual, morally bankrupt gurus.

The older generation (of which I am a part) has given up this country by default. It is not that anyone did the wrong thing; it is simply that we did nothing. We passed on nothing And cared for nothing. If it wasn't going to cost such a devastating price for our offspring, it would be almost funny in a terribly, terribly sad way. The land of the free has become the land of the unrestrained. Welcome back to Rome before Christ (BC). The destruction—a pox on all their houses—will simply be the natural outcome. Anything left unattended will just naturally go to hell—a bunch of nominal moralists standing for absolutely nothing to the death of a generation and a nation.

Chapter 8

A Crooked Generation: Planting a Crop for Harvest

My wife Paulette and I began volunteering at our local county jail in 1994. We both were members of Chuck Colson's "Prison Fellowship" organization, which is a Christian-based ministry aimed at helping those who find themselves at odds with societal laws, personal integrity, and a morality that is not simply relative ethics. The organization's goal is to help these individuals rethink their lifestyle choices and hopefully to renew their minds out of the darkness in which they have lived and seemly found their happiness and fulfillment.

In 1991, Paulette and I were both novices in regard to understanding the depth to which society had fallen when it came to stamping out any idea that there is indeed a right and wrong way to think and act. It seems that if individuals don't learn anything else while in the public school system, the one thing they do learn is that ethics and morals are strictly relative to the individual. This is again reinforce for the lucky few who don't self-destruct but actually go on to some school of higher education. The absurdity that passes for moral and ethical education in many/most of the colleges and universities in the United States at this time is reflected in the unethical actions that seem to be normal in some of the larger and now bankrupt corporations listed on the New York Stock Exchange.

Where did these individuals actually come from? In my opinion, they were raised that way and then educated to think in line with their foundational paradigms. It is not my intent to give a discourse on the destruction sown in the 1960s with regard to the inevitable harvest we are experiencing in this country today. I am not interested in those who have gone on to become the morally corrupt judges, lawyers, stock brokers, and CEOs who are raping the country and the economy at this particular time. The population I am interested in is the population I deal with on a daily basis.

The nominal parenting that was propagated by the generation that grew up in the '60s, spurred on by the so-called experts of the time period, was nothing short of an atheistic abortion of common sense. Common sense seems to be synonymous with religious values, and thus was discarded. Sadly, it is still going on today in courts and educational establishments across America. My concern is for those who have fallen into the clutches of a penal system that turns out individuals who are no better off when they are released than they were when they entered the system. The county jails are no more than the old woodsheds without the belts or straps. There is too little correction administered too late and the wrong kind of programs to boot. So what do you do with a population that is steeped in drug abuse, alcohol abuse, sexual abuse, physical abuse, and just has absolutely no hope for the future? Are they all just stupid or simply not teachable?

I have never actually met someone in the course of my volunteer work within the county penal system over the past seventeen years who did not have some redeeming qualities. Secular programs have utility only as far as they restore correct values and self-respect in the thinking of each individual within the correctional system; there are absolute values and a definite moral code of conduct that are beneficial for all members of society, and those morals are not subjective but rather absolutely empirical and obvious by the outcome of adherence to the principles set forth within the legal system based on Christian values and moral absolutes. The Constitution is a document that is designed to govern a people who have a solid moral foundation. To say that Christian principles should have no place in law because they dictate a doctrine of discipline that is merely arbitrary religious dogma imposed on people who don't want to be governed by such principles but rather want an anything-goes kind of society is to shipwreck the United States and turn it over to a pagan worldview that is polluted with the filth of self-fulfillment and abuse.

Chapter 9

Writing on the Wall: Why Bother?

Everybody is somebody's baby. Then they grow up a little and go to public schools, which are staffed in large part by secular humanists, who themselves are a product of this never-ending circle of deception and decay. If you are amazed at the greed that is so prevalent within American society and the subsequent problems being experienced within corporate America today, you have only yourself to blame. The passivity that the populous in America today expresses through its inaction is paramount to depraved indifference toward those who must live here in the future, and that is a criminal offense.

The prison population today has been brought up within a corrupt society, and now the caregivers who are in place over them exhibit behaviors and attitudes that have helped the prisoners become exactly what they have become: self-centered, looking-out-for-number-one, get-it-while-you-can, live-for-the-moment, hedonistic individuals. This attitude expresses itself in many different stages of individual development. Most of the individuals at the county jail level were quick to jump into this self-serving behavior for instant gratification with no regard or awareness of future consequences. Others held off on totally destructive behavior because of an awareness of the importance of education and training in regard to future successful financial attainment. This awareness must have been instilled by parents with at least some degree of social awareness of the need to comply with social norms in order for a culture to actually continue and thus offer the opportunity to fulfill individual hedonistic dreams.

Most individuals in our county jails have very small dreams and settle for momentary satisfaction of personal goals that are so temporary that it is not a real surprise that most of these prisoners are in need of general equivalence diplomas (GEDs). The simpleminded have simple goals. Not surprisingly, these individuals are quite sure that they are smart. Yes, it is true that most of these individuals come from environments where the people who raised them were exactly the same as their offspring. That is not to say that all the parents of this group are as morally depraved as the prisoners are. Indeed, some parents try to instill some socially acceptable character qualities in their children, but as their children spend more time with morally relative teachers and secular entertainment hedonists, it really is a losing battle. So what then is rehabilitation?

It never ceases to amaze me that anything that may actually seem like common sense or strategies for the betterment of society are attacked on the grounds that they are religious in nature and therefore separate from the guidelines for proper social behavior. Those who shout the loudest are the groups that have actually made it out of adolescence with an eye on financial prosperity and free moral depravity while putting off instant self-gratification for the hope of experiencing these hedonistic opportunities in the penthouses instead of under a bridge in a cardboard box. The federal courts have to deal with this group, but the local community ends up dealing with the weakest minded of the losers. So the question once again is, why bother?

Well, the answer is that these people actually do breed on impulse in an alerted state of mind with no regard for the consequences. Sexual intercourse is nothing more than a ride at the carnival. Like a day at the park, the idea is to get on as many rides as possible. The number of individuals in the county jails who have several children from several different females (and vice versa) and who have never been married is mind-boggling. All the females are on public assistance, and then the state charges the fathers for their support. Oh, good idea. This population that is uneducated, has no skills, and is bound in both alcohol and substance addictions is really going to be able to get out of this debt. That is not very likely.

Let me say in no uncertain terms that it is my opinion that "freedom of religion" as stated in our Constitution was a given by our founding fathers to mean freedom of worship and belief within the context of Christianity. Our founding fathers did not in their wildest dreams ever think this fact even needed to be stated. This country was founded on Christian scriptural precepts. One only has to go back and study the early documents, which were the foundation of this idea of democracy, to see the truth. The founding fathers of these United States never could have imagined the intellectual depravity that would seep into the moral thinking of the populous and thus allow the election to public office of like-minded hedonistic utopian leaders, void of any understanding of moral absolutes.

These Darwinian cultists now infect every aspect of American leadership, from school teachers and college professors to the judges on our Supreme Court. Our leadership is a direct product of the dysfunctional educational system within the United States. This educational system was originally founded on the Christian scriptures and worked well for a long time until the social intellectuals decided we were much too bright to need any guidelines for survival as a people. We are now reaping the depraved teachings of the '60s, '70s, and '80s. The morally devoid children of that era are now our professors, judges, and legislators. The number of depraved, indifferent individuals is accelerating in geometric proportions; we are pumping these individuals out in record numbers.

The intelligent individuals go on to corporate corruption, and local communities are left with the GED crowd. The early alcoholics and drug addicts who are brain dead before the age of thirteen go on to become the petty thieves and local drug dealers. Unfortunately these people never leave the local communities. They are the revolving-door crowd of both the local jails and the local mental health clinics.

Chapter 10

Christian Virtue in American Society: A Categorical Imperative

American society is being murdered from within. The very foundational thinking that has supported it for over two hundred years is being willfully denied in the public forum. The federal government of the United States of America is bound by duty to protect its citizens and allow—no, encourage—the proclamation of Christian values in the public arena.

The fact that a particular standard is good for society and has proven its worth as a stabilizing force among good (virtuous) men does not in itself make these standards a religious doctrine. The Constitution of this country states "that *Congress* shall pass no law establishing a religion …" (author's emphasis). The expression of religious values does not establish anything except a citizen with moral convictions.

In John Stuart Mill's writing on the ethical theory of utilitarianism, he states, "Actions are right in proportion as they tend to promote happiness, wrong as they tend to produce the reverse" (Mill, 1995, 95). According to Mill, "good" means happiness, and happiness means pleasure and the absence of pain (Mill, 1995,95). As a society, America is in a great deal of pain, yet the government (state) insists that teaching morals in public education is somehow unconstitutional. The government insists that teaching moral absolutes is teaching religion. It is unethical for a governing body to eliminate the teaching of morals to its next generation. The principles of the upcoming generation become the basis for the laws which this generation will enact. A generation of leaders with no moral values is doomed to destroy the people they lead.

"If any opinion is compelled to silence, that opinion may, for aught we can certainly know, be true. To deny this is to assume our own infallibility" (Mill, 1995, 139). "If we are Christian and a senator, our votes and actions might be different than if we were atheist and a senator, but while we may conduct our lives according to our religious beliefs, the Constitution forbids a state established church But where and how we draw the line between church and state is not particularly clear. There is also no question that the law is significantly influenced by morality" (Locke, 1995, 101). Actually the Constitution does not have any such verbiage in regard to church and state—only that there should be no religion officially established as a governmental entity.

A person is who he is! You can't tell a person to make judgments and that in doing so he should exclude what he believes is right from his thinking. In a word, moral states are the results of activities corresponding to the moral states themselves. If a statesman is moral in his activities and brings these moral attitudes into his government decisions, is he establishing a religion, or is he performing his duty as a statesman? I believe he is indeed doing his duty as he was elected to do it. If a politician has no concept of moral principles, should he be made to adopt moral principles so that he doesn't establish a religion of atheism? That would be nonsense. To exclude what is conceived of as religious principles from the policymaking decisions of an elected representative of the people is to deny those things that the people recognized as the essence and character of the man. "The good man out of the good treasures of his heart brings forth good things, and an evil man out of the evil treasure brings forth evil things" (Matt 12:35, NKJV). "For out of the abundance of the heart the mouth speaks" (Matt 12:34, NKJV).

Immanuel Kant, in his writing *The Fundamental Principles of the Metaphysics of Morals*, states that "nothing can be called good without qualification, except a good will" (Kant, 1995, 83).

To do the right thing when we can is the duty of all men and the duty of the state. Just because the right thing is also considered right in the light of "religious" belief does not effectively establish a religion, even if the individual expressing this opinion is an elected official. Even if every elected official were Christian and made decisions based on his or her beliefs, no official religion is established. The people in a democracy can change their elected officials at any time, and Congress has made no law establishing a religion.

Christian virtues are for the bigger good within the society. "It is better to be a human being dissatisfied than a pig satisfied; better to be Socrates dissatisfied then a fool satisfied. And if the fool or the pig is of a different opinion, it is because they only know their own side of the question. The other party to the comparison knows both sides" (Mill, 1995, 98)

Not allowing Christian principles back into our society as foundational supports for democracy is the equivalent to not allowing the inhabitants of this society to express their values through the statesmen they elect. By the same perverted interpretation of church and state, we are establishing secular humanism as the nation's religious foundation.

It is my strong belief that this country is at a crossroads in history: life or death. Democracy can only survive and can only be effective for its populace, if that populace is a moral people. The humanist push for "freedom" while having no Christian consensus to contain it causes that "freedom" to lead to chaos or to slavery under the state (or under an elite). Humanism, with its lack of any final basis for values or law, always leads to chaos (Schaefffer, 1981, 29).

To illustrate this point, one only needs to look at the condition of society since God was thrown out of the public school system in 1962. There was a time when the biggest problems in the public educational system were chewing gum and talking in class, and occasionally a young lady would go to visit her relatives for nine months. Now, thirty years later, problems range from assaults on teachers to rape and murder for a pair of sneakers. One does not need to quote an endless array of statistics; statistics can be misrepresented. Just pick up any newspaper and the stench of death will flood off the pages into the very heart of any virtuous (good) man.

I am thankful that there seems to be a turning tide in this country. Good (virtues) people are starting to demand a change in the political correctness of the government. Religious values are being brought back to the public forum. People who hold religious values are demanding, and getting the right to speak from a Christian viewpoint. Bible clubs have regained their right to form and meet in our public schools. Student-led prayer is once again permitted on school property, and the passing out of Christian literature is no longer censored in public schools.

William J. Bennett's book, titled *The Book of Virtues*, is now being used in the school system. In the introduction on page 13, Bennett says,

> *... the task of teaching moral literacy and forming character is not political in the usual meaning of the term. People of good character are not all going to come down on the same side of difficult political and social issues. Good people—people of character and moral literacy—can be conservative, and good people can be liberal.*

It's the foundation that makes a difference! On March 9, 1790, Benjamin Franklin wrote to Ezra Stiles, president of Yale University:

"Here is my Creed. I believe in one God, the Creator of the Universe. That He governs it by His Providence. That He ought to be worshipped. That the most acceptable service we render to Him is in doing good to His other children. That the soul of man is immortal, and will be treated with Justice in another Life respecting its conduct in this. These I take to be the fundamental points in all sound Religion, and I regard them as you do in whatever Sect I meet with them. As to Jesus of Nazareth, my Opinion of whom you particularly desire, I think the System of Morals and his Religion, as he left them to us, is the best the World ever saw, or is likely to see."

Section III

He who finds a wife finds a good thing, And obtains favor from the Lord.

—Proverbs 18:22, NKJV

Husbands, love your wives, just as Christ also loved the church and gave Himself for her.

—Ephesians 5:25, NKJV

Husbands, love your wives and do not be bitter toward them.

— Colossians 3:19, NKJV

Chapter 11

Women Have a Legitimate Gripe: Where Is the Love and Respect?

See to it that no one carries you off as spoil or makes you yourselves captive by his so-called philosophy and intellectualism and vain deceit (idle fancies and plain nonsense), following human tradition (men's ideas of the material rather than the spiritual world), just crude notions following the rudimentary and elemental teachings of the universe and disregarding [the teachings of] Christ (the Messiah).

— Colossians 2:8 (AMP)

An old perspective with a common objective

It's funny how my wife found it humorous when I said that I had gained a wonderful understanding of what wives have been going through for a very long time in regard to thinking their husbands are insensitive to their needs for companionship. Being a househusband has given me a unique male perspective on the issue, actually a kind of crossover view. It may well be true that the husband does not even know that this concern of the female homemaker is based in reality and not some type of neurosis.

As for me, I have been a househusband for more than twenty years.

It was a role reversal I accepted quite willingly. Having also been in the restaurant business for over a decade, cooking and cleaning were not concepts with which I was unfamiliar. A few years in the U.S. Navy did not hinder me in the areas of self-discipline and commitment to duty. Frankly, it actually established those traits into my personality.

A homemaker, housewife, mother, caregiver—what do these terms really mean? Some are given in the politically correct version so as not to give the impression of some cultural expectation. I suppose that serves a purpose in the minds of the kill-Barbie-and-Ken generation. It is not my intent to be politically correct. My observations of the "keeper of the castle" are strictly observations made by a male focused on and responsive to the traditionally female domain: the home.

For all of those people who think that the idea of homemaker has been culturally thrust upon the female gender, I would only say this: females are genetically predisposed to actually take on this task and survive somewhat mentally intact. It is with this in mind that I would appeal to men in our society. You will notice I did not say males. All men are born males, but not all males ever truly become men. To pay heed to some of the simplest of observations that have penetrated my heart and mind while functioning in this role as househusband, I would like to share some of the insights I have gained in regard to what is needed to bring an uplifting expressed appreciation of all that the housewife brings to the traditional marital relationship.

Not all men are lucky enough to find a woman who is secure enough in her own heart and mind to actually tackle the idea of being a housewife. Women have been deceived into thinking they must be independent of men, and having believed this fallacy, they have wasted countless years pursuing careers that have only shortened their life spans and made them more susceptible to the maladies that have generally been the domain of males striving to survive.

Quite frankly, if I were a young girl just entering into puberty and suddenly came to realize what was expected of me by mother nature and society in regard to childbearing and the main position in the rearing of these little creatures, I would run away into some kind of career myself. It is my belief that most young girls are not necessarily seeking an education as they are an abdication from their natural purpose and calling in life, and they are taught this philosophy by those who would like to have some control over population expansion within the world. Oh yes, baby factories dominated by ugly slave-driving males.

Some males may participate in some really dysfunctional relationships with women, thinking of them as their servants and not truly understanding the wonderful companionship women and men can offer one another across a lifetime of friendship. Many males and females live in close proximity to one another, inflicting endless amounts of pain and suffering on one another and their offspring.

It is not to this last group that I address myself. These folks are better served as clients in some free clinic dealing with spousal abuse. It is to those whom I would call "simply frustrated" or "fellow sojourners" that I endeavor to share what has become impressed on my thoughts and has influenced my behavior in regard to my relationship with a woman who has graciously accepted me as her lifelong companion in a Christ-centered relationship.

How can anyone deny that females are indeed hardwired a little differently than males? Some individuals would argue the point that this difference is strictly dictated by the culture within which a female has been raised—cultural expectations, so to speak. This point cannot be disputed, but in my opinion, it is not the only reason for said differences between males and females. Nurture plays an important role in the development of individuals, but there are also basic fundamental differences in the biochemical makeup of both males and females that, try as hard as your political correctness dictates, cannot be disputed.

Men and women are equal in their capacity for any cognitive achievement, though their perspectives may be slightly skewed in regard to any given schema of personal perspective. Women are merely men with a womb, and this biological fact dictates some natural consequences. Like it or not, only women can give birth. This is a fact, even as much as some misguided women find this to be a form of entrapment to biological mandates and seek to somehow find another way to procreate in the hopes of freeing themselves from any dependence on males. This abdication of their biological responsibility in this physical existence is sadly a response to many of the dysfunctional patterns of many males within the many cultures of world today. There are simply too many men who do not understand the God-given blessing of a faithful woman in a faithful man's life, a woman who is committed to a family unit in the hopes of raising children, securing a home, building a hopeful future together, and having another human being to trust, love, and grow old with. Nor do they know the blessing of a relationship in which they protect one another from all the mental ills and temptations that can be brought on by hopelessness, emptiness, and the feeling of being alone in this existence with no real hope of finding the elusive dream of happiness.

Now, it has been said that women are the weaker vessel. In regard to their physical capacity for athletic performance, this may in fact be a true statement. This is not a put-down of a woman's ability to accomplish goals of performance that are far above an untrained male's ability to accomplish. It is only in comparison of a female athlete to a highly trained male athlete within the same sport or activity that there are differences in peak performance capabilities.

Actually, the statement that women are the weaker vessel refers to the emotional context and not in a derogatory way either. Women are only weaker in the respect that they are more wonderfully made, much as a fine piece of artwork is fashioned to show off a craftsman's ability to work with delicate material to create beauty and stir emotional responses in the hearts of those who behold his fragile, beautiful creation. The creation is not weak in a demeaning way; rather it is more fragile and should be handled with care. This is something many egotistical males have not a clue about in regard to how to correctly understand a relationship with a woman. A woman—the man with the womb—is equal in all ways to the male except for some general physical capacity relative to size and training. She is just simply more fragile in the context of emotional sensitivities. Some environmental aspects of growing up within certain cultures may have purposefully been designed to cause some individuals to think that being male is somehow better than being female. Many home and public environments try to push a form of being equal but separate on both males and females to the distraction of both genders. Do you remember the unisex clothing era?

Before you begin to think it is my opinion that women should be barefoot and pregnant and not be allowed to pursue their own destinies in the realm of education and professional endeavors, I would simply respond that it is not the case. But it is the reality that only one of the genders actually can carry and give birth to children. Sorry about that. When woman was created, it was indeed with a purpose in mind, and it wasn't for her to push off childbearing into a test tube. It was to be a help to her mate and bear children.

Fake it till you make it

Being a caring mate requires some cognitive activity beyond our concerns for our own little worlds. Love is not a feeling; it is an active desire of one's own will to be directed toward another whom at times may not actually be all that lovable. And, yes, by mate I do mean the other half of a marital contract between a female and a male who are committed to journey through life together with all the traditional trappings: a home, children, shared financial responsibility, and a shared commitment to stick it out through thick and thin (for better or for worse).

Now some of the foundational thinking necessary for the harmony of this type of relationship will certainly work to enhance other perverse types of relationships simply because the principles of caring for another person in your life are fundamentally desirable for all one-on-one relationships.

So what does "fake it till you make it" actually mean? Well, this term can be found in Alcoholics Anonymous (AA), and I presume it is applicable to any desired behavior a person is pursuing and having difficulty establishing in his or her life. At the turn of the century (that is the late 1800s to the twentieth century), a psychologist named William James said that in order to change behavioral habits, you should "act the way you want to be," regardless of the struggles you may face in order to become the way you want to be. In other words, fake it till you make it.

One would presume that in order to do this "thing," one would have to have a desired behavior in mind to begin with. One might ask on what basis an individual might decide he wants to change a particular behavior in his accommodating schemas of so many ways of acting and reacting to others in his life. Well, one might want to change behaviors that have proven destructive or at the very least nonproductive in reaching a harmonious relationship with a spouse.

As a male who is on the other side of the traditional fence of gender expectations within a culture, I have come to realize that most of the static from the housewife, homemaker, foundation of the relationship, are grounded in fact. The person leaving the house to go off to work and the person left at the house to work really are mostly at odds except when they both have the ability to appreciate one another. Can you learn to appreciate the other in a truly loving, non-self-centered (what-is-in-it-for-me) attitude? Can you learn to become the person you want to become and defeat self-defeating behaviors and ingrained attitudes? You can, once you establish the way you want to be and then fake it till you make it.

It takes a desire to be pleasing to another

And what does that mean, to be pleasing to another? Why should we be concerned about altering our own selves in some manner simply to be pleasing to our mates? Well, quite simply, if the mate is in a pleasant disposition because they are "pleased" as in "happy," "comfortable," and "cognitively soothed," he or she is more receptive to the idea of putting down his or her ego and simply becoming his or her non-self-protective self.

We as individuals are generally on guard against being ourselves because we are so unfamiliar with the "real" us. Walk in love! No more plastic smiles or personas. So many people have been so self-protective for so long that they really don't even begin to know what it is to be open to another person and not only let down their shields but put their shields in the closet and put a smile on their hearts.

Men and women belong together in this reality to create more of the human race for the future. When you read that men and women get married and become one flesh, it is not only talking about a physical union, for indeed you give a part of yourself with a physical encounter, but the only true one flesh from two individuals is the DNA of the children they produce. When you read that "I knew you before you were in your mother's womb," it gives you some understanding of how awesome the Creator of the universe really is. He knows every possible combination of DNA there could ever be and the person that it would create. We are all in fact made in His image when it comes to the spirit that is created from these unions. Love your wife. Respect your husband.

The risk is worth the payback you receive when you have the right person living in your heart of hearts to help you not only to love unconditionally but also to love with no expectation of reward for your efforts. It's not about what you can get but rather about what you can give. It really is more rewarding to give than to receive. I have it on good authority from a Man who knows.

Chapter 12

The Essence of Love: What Happened to Us as Men?

I was occupying my time just the other day doing little household chores and thinking about nothing in particular. The laundry was washed, dried, and folded. The vacuuming was done, and the kitchen floor was swept and washed. I found myself thinking about how much I loved and cared for my wife. It was just a fleeting thought, and it made me smile.

I had been to prison just the other day, and the men's faces always seem to parade before me for a couple of days after such encounters. The old, the young—all those souls coming out for Bible study. Some come just to get off the blocks. Others are looking for relief from the bondage of their minds and their confusion over life and its purpose. I've never sat with an incarcerated man or woman who I did not find to be oh-so-much like myself in so many ways. I guess the sense of these feelings is what you might call their humanity. They always make me smile, and they always make me cry. Did you ever cry and not know why? It can be a very perplexing feeling when something inside of you swells up from your heart and causes all your senses to contort your countenance into an expression of sadness, with all the tears and muffled groans that signify some unknown grief.

It seems that of late, I have become susceptible to situations that evoke these emotions. Well, maybe that is not really what I mean. I sense I have always been aware of these sensitivities but have kept them in check by design. What is that all about, I wonder? I had once heard a professional dramatic artist say that the purpose of drama was to stir up the emotions of the people watching. To draw them into situations that would "touch their hearts," so to speak, in a particular manner purposefully designed to do just that.

That is an interesting concept and goal, to want to facilitate people's experiences of certain emotions. It would seem that the emotions of individuals are designed for a purpose, given to us for a reason, and natural to all mankind. Our individual hot buttons can be pushed by the circumstances of everyday living and our interactions with other humans; it is my opinion, that the more consistent the contact with the other person, the "hotter" the buttons can get. The song lyric that states, "You always hurt the one you love," should more aptly say, "You can really only hurt the one that loves you." And that could be qualified by saying, only in the realm of a wound of the heart. The feeling of betrayal is felt at the core of your soul.

It is easy to make a stranger angry with you, either intentionally or inadvertently. But you can only really wound someone in his or her heart when there is a deep emotional attachment and a feeling of unity and trust betrayed. The fabric of our hearts can endure many onslaughts of minor acquaintances and come through unscathed. It is only when the perpetrator has been woven into our hearts and souls through love that the fabric has no defense. How about you? Do you really love anybody? I mean *really* love someone? Do you love your wife? Do you love your husband? Do you love your boyfriend or girlfriend? And if the answer is yes, why do you love them? How about your children? Do you love them?

Do you recognize the humanity of other human beings? To see the same essence in another human being that is in you is to understand how similar we all are to one another. We are all human, made in the image of God. Compassion and mercy are the offspring of love. No real love, no real compassion, just good intentions founded on a philosophy of presumed altruistic motivation. To do something and then feel good about it is not the same as simply feeling good about doing something with forethought. One is gratifying to the self, and the other is self-gratification, respectively.

Without a revelation of humanity, and the oneness of the whole human race, we are shipwrecked on the rocks of indifference and mediocrity. Only being able to express true love for another person specifically and to the world corporately can you emotionally fulfill your soul. Can you love unconditionally if you have never experienced true unconditional love? Probably not. You may express many of the counterfeit emotional expressions that were at some point directed at you that you perceived as love.

Counterfeits look a whole lot like the real thing, but they are eventually exposed for what they truly are when they fail to hold up under close examination or fail to perform as the original was designed to perform. Counterfeits are only vague images of the real thing. They have no worth. One thing that is good about counterfeits is that they are very obvious when you have known the real thing. Do you know how they train bank tellers to identify counterfeit money? They expose them to endless handling of the real thing. When a counterfeit comes along, they recognize it immediately. Sadly, most people are so familiar with counterfeit emotions that when the real thing comes along, they question its validity. When real love comes along, they try to seek out the motive behind its expression.

What does it mean to love another human being? Why would you love another human being? Why would you want to love another human being? Is it for what you could get, or is it for what you could give? Is it really better to give than to receive, and if so, why? Jesus can explain it to you in His Father's Word. Come and read. Renew your mind, and experience what real love actually feels like. Then you won't settle for the world's counterfeit. (See Appendix A)

Chapter 13

Decisive Living over Default Apathy: Time Flies and the Outward Man Dies

One day you turn around and you find that life and time are passing by at an alarming rate. So I thought I would take a reality check and see exactly how I "really" felt about my present location on the time line of my life. As I consider the fact that I am actually not as young as I used to be, it is quite a revelation. I mean, I counsel with men ranging in age from seventeen-year-old "juvies" to men from my cohort group and everybody in between—young and old, tall and short, thin and fat, with and without hair, with teeth and some with only a couple of tusk-like protrusions that hold onto the bridgework. From self-professed philosophers to down-and-out street dwellers, we all have one thing for sure in common and that is the fact that we are all getting older day by day.

Some carry their years on their faces better than others. Drugs and alcohol and just hard-thought or hard-fought lives will put the wrinkles on your face. I guess that is why they call some wrinkles "worry lines" and some of them "smile lines" and others "laugh lines." Whichever the lines may be, they make up the tapestry of our countenance, depending on which emotion we put forth from our inner man at any given moment in time.

It isn't really true that you are only as young as you feel. The reality is that you are only as old as you think within your mind's eye. My wife and I have lived in this particular dwelling for over twenty years now. When I was thirty-nine, I was roaming around this house doing the everyday things we all do in our homes. Though we come and go from this destination, we don't always realize the passing of time in its insidious, never-ending march forward. Time marks decay. It is time that generates the passing away of material items, and the human experience is dependent upon time. Time is like a flowing stream; it comes at us from the future, passes over us in the moment, and proceeds toward what becomes the past or history of our lives.

Yet, at each stage of our lives these periods of time are all connected by a thin fabric of our existence; we are connected to the past, not the past that lies behind us but the one that lies perpendicular to us, the one at our right and left, our children and grandchildren who will/have come after us. They are the ones who make the reality of passing time have such an impact on our own sense of reality. Once they didn't even exist, then they were here with us, and now they are growing older, and there is nothing we can do to mark time and stay in place. We move forward as they chase us into old age in order to live their own lives as adults.

Time keeps coming until it will indeed push us into an existence that is beyond this physical life. Many people have had philosophical opinions over the centuries to try to explain the whole meaning of existence or life (you can take your pick as to what you would call it yourself). Some people are too lazy to give it much thought; they just live it and die. Some just live it and die long before they are actually dead. They walk and talk, but the lights are out and nobody is home. For these people, life ceases to have meaning long before the chronological timeframe would indicate as a time of closure. Dead but alive, a failure to thrive!

It is sad to see how many people would simply rather live an empty life of their own choosing than an abundant life governed by the schemas and attitudes that have to be purposefully developed through hard work and dedication to purpose. It seems the default is always easier to lean back on. It really takes no effort whatsoever; you just have to breathe, eat, and sleep. The rest of your life just happens by circumstantial events that don't happen to destroy you: good luck and bad luck. I'll take well-thought-out blessings over luck any day. The purposeful, absolutely *on purpose* opinions and precepts that are accepted with a conscious mind working toward a life that is open to the blessings of God to be poured out on His children because of their willingness to receive His Love and His direction in their lives is what sets the stage for what some people may call living with the favor of God in your life.

Appendix A

An Amazing Nine Minutes

It really is an amazing fact of life that in reality we are all in this creation alone as human beings. We are all very much the same in so many ways, but those ways are mostly superficial. I mean, we are all basically designed the same way in regards to our physiological needs and functions, but inside our psyches where it really counts, we are all as different from one another as the stars in the evening sky.

Exactly the same but different! It sounds like a contradiction. Everyone knows you can't be two opposite things at the same time. Well, the difference lies in the unseen aspects of the human experience. It lies in the part of us that is developing every day through how we perceive circumstances and how we apply what we observe to ourselves in relation to its relevance to our situations. It depends on whether the things we perceive are merely observed and then either stored in memory or dismissed as irrelevant in our particular circumstance.

With all the individuals who we come in contact with over our lifetimes, there is not one who shares our life experiences with us in the same manner that we experience him or her on our own personal level. No manner of explanation can ever convey to another exactly the way we "feel." We try to convey these things through poems, songs, philosophies, expressions, or particular continence. Now, even though we are all similar in design, there is one difference that isn't just subjective in nature; it is the X and Y chromosomes that distinguish us from one another on a level of real physical differences within the human species. The human condition is in many ways on a level of observable similarities, most obviously a contradiction as well in areas that are most notably gender specific.

Some people seem to think that this difference doesn't necessarily manifest itself in the area of psychological differences in regard to emotional expression and just plain old femininity and masculinity due to testosterone and estrogen excretions from the organs that signify our gender.

Speaking as a male who has always been fascinated by the sheer delight to be found in any close relationship with a female, I must say that women are amazing creatures.

During the course of relationship management, we all have come to anticipate the needs and desires of someone with whom we are closely tied to, either spiritually or merely physically. To be in close proximity in our everyday lives to someone of a different genetic persuasion can be a challenge at best or confusing at its worst.. There are all kinds of observations that have been made about the way women react to one another and the way men don't react to one another except in superficial ways. I have heard it said that women are fine-print people and men are strictly headline people. This may be true to some extent, but I would put forth that it isn't always true in a meaningful relationship between two individuals of the opposite sex.

I believe that there are times when both parties seek to get closer to the other but somehow manage to get in each other's way. There have been many psychological theories about avoidance and the "approach and withdraw" theories of personal relationships, but many are nothing more than mere observational conjectures or input from the test subjects themselves. I mean never ask the thing what it thinks about itself. It doesn't know anything about the subject matter; it doesn't know its own purpose. How can it suggest a hypothesis on someone else's behavior or reasoning objectives?

I find that it can be difficult to stay one step ahead of my wife in this regard. I say wife because without a real, life-long commitment to someone else, one can never really trust the motives of oneself and definitely not the motives of someone who might be here today and gone tomorrow depending on how the mood moves him or her on that particular day. Commitment is the only thing that will open the door to another's soul and actually give you a peek into the inner workings of the command center that directs the body you sleep next to every night and long to hold every day of your life. That is love, and that is commitment: one body, one soul, together as one couple, holding on to one another as you pass through this existence we call our physical life spans.

When you are always looking forward to seeing the other person and your heart leaps a little when he or she comes into view, it is a great feeling to experience—love. And when he or she smiles back, you understand that it is a great feeling to be loved, not for a moment in time but for your lifetime. In the good times and in the hard times, you have a friend to hold close, to anchor your feelings and hopes in, who is another part of you.

It can be tough to get to spend quality time together. If one is not on the run, the other one is about to get lost in the thoughts for the day or the thoughts for tomorrow. If one is up, the other is busy; if one is down, the other is distracted by life and its many avenues of distraction. When can you ever find time to just simply have a nonsexual or emotionally non-tumultuous moment of interaction that isn't stimulus overload on every occasion? There is a time when the variables are not all present and the shields are down in successive intervals of time. That can be a wonderful time of total control without any resistance to the affection we all long to express in an honest way, without guards on duty to offer a countenance of skepticism, their eyes darting with curiosity masked in unbelief.

When a male offers sincerity to a female, even if it is a male who is committed to her and she believes in his commitment, her response is often guarded at best and resistant at worst. You have to catch the lady in the nine-minute window of the snooze alarm. It can be the most amazing nine minutes if you catch her just right.

To begin with, the clock has to be on your side of the bed, and you need to let it *beep* (yes, *beep*) for about five seconds before you hit the snooze. This allows her to come out of sleepyland just enough to be in that realm of defenselessness and little girl snuggly. You remember, kind of like the hamster in the cedar chips when as a child you use to tickle its ears while it was sleeping and it would wiggle a little and twitch its nose but never open its eyes; it's cute as a button and so trusting, as if it were in the arms of its Creator. Well, wives can be that way also when caught in that nine-minute window of bliss where the cares of this world are blurred by the slumber of a soul at rest. You can hold her close, and she won't squirm away. You can gently rub her head or message her scalp and the back of her neck and you get a purring sound in return instead of her usual "don't mess my hair up." You can smell her hair and yesterday's perfume without having a fight to stop wasting time. It really can be an amazing nine minutes.

When it is over, you can be the first one up, get the alarm, put on the light, say good morning, and head for the coffee pot to have it ready for her when she appears on the scene to take up her spot in her chair. It is funny how the emotional calmness that showed up in the nine-minute window can sometimes extend over into the rest of the day. I think it has to do with a trust realized and the comfort of closeness without the defensiveness that develops over a lifetime of vigilance; it can be an amazing nine minutes.

Fight for your right to show yourself as faithful and as a man of honor who simply loves to love with a never-ending compassion based not in the physical aspects of the union but rather in the truly spiritual realm of a true union of souls.

House and riches are the inheritance from fathers, but a wise, understanding, and prudent wife is from the Lord.

—Proverbs 19:14 AMP

He who finds a [true] wife finds a good thing and obtains favor from the Lord.

—Proverbs 18:22 AMP

A capable, intelligent, and virtuous woman—who is he who can find her? She is far more precious than jewels and her value is far above rubies or pearls.

— Proverbs 31:10 AMP

Appendix B

The Good News

John 3:16

For God so loved the world, that he gave his only begotten Son, that whosoever believeth in him should not perish, but have everlasting life.

King James Version

John 3:16

For God so loved the world that He gave His only begotten Son, that whoever believes in Him should not perish but have everlasting life.

New King James Version

John 3:16

This is how much God loved the world: He gave his Son, his one and only Son. And this is why: so that no one need be destroyed; by believing in him, anyone can have a whole and lasting life.

John 3:16

For God loved the world so much that he gave his one and only Son, so that everyone who believes in him will not perish but have eternal life.

Bibliography

Deuteronomy 18:10, Old Testament Christian Bible NKJV

Douglass, Frederick. April 28, 1845. *Narrative of the Life of Frederick Douglass, An American Slave.* Lynn, MA.

Engel, S. Morris, With Good Reason, AN INTRODUCTION TO INFORMAL FALLACIES, Fifth Edition, St. Martins Press Inc., NY, NY, 1994, page 50

James, William, HERBENHANHN, B.R., An introduction to the to the History of Psychology, Third Addition, BROOKS/COLE PUBLISHING COMPANY 1997, Pacific Grove, CA, page 307

Kant, Immanuel, Critique of Practical Reason, Foley & Mohan, Marywood College, Scranton, PA, Philosophical Inquiry an introduction, ALBE HOUSE, NY, NY, 1995, page 74

Kant, Immanuel, The Fundamental Principles of the Metaphysics of Morals, Foley & Mohan, Pimis, Marywood College, 1995 page 83

Lewin, Kurt, HERGENHANHN, B.R., An Introduction to the History of Psychology, Third Addition, BROOKS/COLE PUBLISHING COMPANY, 1997, Pacific Grove, CA, page 423

Locke, John, Second Treatise of Government, Foley & Mohan,

Philosophical Inquiry, an introduction, Marywood College, ALBA HOUSE, NY, NY, 1995, page 101

Matthew 12:35, Holy Bible New King James Version

Matthew 12:34, Holy Bible, New King James Version

Mesmer, Franz, HERGENHANHN, B.R., An introduction to the History of Psychology, Third Addition, BROOKS/COLE PUBLISHING COMPANY, 1997, Pacific Grove, CA, page 449

Mill, John Stuart, Utilitarianism, (published serially in Frazer's Magazine in 1861) Foley & Mohan, Primis, Marywood College, McGraw Hill Inc. 1995, page 95

Mill, John Stuart, Utilitarianism, (published serially in Frazer's Magazine in 1861) Foley & Mohan, Primis, Marywood College, McGraw Hill Inc. 1995, page 98

Mill, John Stuart, On Liberty, 1859, Foley & Mohan, Marywood College, Scranton, PA, Primis, 1995, page 139

New Merriam-Webster Dictionary1989, G.K. Hall & Co

Piaget, J, Psychology of intelligence, 1966, Totowa, NJ, Littlefield & Adams, Hergenhahn, B.R. & Matthew, H. Olson, An Introduction To Theories Of Learning, Fifth Edition, Prentice Hall, 1997, Upper Saddle River, NJ 07458, page 282

Pocono Record. April 1, 2009. In Our Opinion: Boys Not Acting Like Boys. 115 (No. 365):A6.

Schaeffer, Dr. Francis A., A Christian Manifesto, Crossway Books a division of Good News Publication in association with Nims Communication, 1981, page 29

Washington, George. September 17, 1796. Farewell Speech.

About the Author

The author was born in New York City in 1946 and moved with his family to Bergen County, New Jersey, shortly thereafter. His parents were divorced when he was eight years old. It could be said that he came from a broken home, though his mother (a registered nurse) did remarry four years later. He has an older sister and a younger brother.

The author's stepfather was a gentle man, but the relationship between them was not that interactive. Except for usual teenage conflicts while growing up, their overall interactions were mostly amicable.

In 1965, the author graduated from high school and joined the United States Navy in September of that year and headed to the Great Lakes Naval Station to attend boot camp. The author credits his military service with instilling in him many qualities that served him well later in his life: duty, attention to detail, the ability to work hard, and alas, the ability to party hard. It is to this last attribute that the author credits many of the difficulties he encountered during the 1970s and early 1980s.

That is not to say there were not some times of victory during that period. In fact, it was in early 1972 that an employee encouraged the author to look at his Christian faith more closely in regard to actually living it instead of simply identifying with it in name only and in a somewhat nominal fashion. This set the stage for a later dedication to what the author has come to learn is a lifestyle worth pursuing—a lifestyle based on a firm foundation of the reality of the validity of the Christian scriptures.

In the mid-1980s, the author came to realize that the obvious things the Christian lifestyle had always steered away from were in fact good things to remove from any healthy lifestyle (e.g., recreational use of alcohol, tobacco, and any other mind-altering substances that are not of some legitimate medical advantage).

In 1990, church attendance introduced the author to Chuck Colson's Prison Fellowship organization. With some training, the author began volunteering to do Bible studies in the local county prison in Monroe County, Pennsylvania, with his wife Paulette. This continued through 1996.

The author was encouraged by a chaplain to take advantage of the opportunity to go to college to gain a better understanding of the problems members of the prison population might be confronting in their lives. It was also during this period that the author began his studies with Rhema Bible College correspondence courses in Tulsa Oklahoma.

In 2000, the author graduated from Marywood University in Scranton, Pennsylvania, with a BS in psychology (*summa cum laude*) and two semesters postgraduate work in mental health counseling. In 2001, the author received his certificate of completion from Rhema Bible College. In 2001, the author once again returned to the county prison, this time in Luzerne County, Pennsylvania, as the chaplain's assistant. He remained in this position until 2008.

Through these many years of biblical counseling with people in distress, the author has formed some opinions about what may be at the root of many of the problems inmates and their families encounter in this present age. It also has become apparent to the author that the problems of this particular group may in fact be a microcosm of the infectious malaise that has crept into the society of the United States as a whole; to the destruction of our culture, our personal integrity, all restraints on personal lustful behavior, and with no concept of duty to others. Our educational system has beaten patriotism and love of sovereignty out of this present generation. These attributes have been drummed out of this present generation in the name of a global citizenship based on secularism and humanistic worldviews.

This book is a culmination of these observations and a call to arms for people of faith to take a stand for the future of the country and the mental health and future happiness of their grandchildren.